D1576822

The
ILLUSTRATED
LAKE
POETS

To Richard and Sylvia Wordsworth, with love.

ON THE ISLAND AT GRASMERE

Rude is this edifice . . . yet to these walls
The heifer comes in the snow-storm, and here
The new-dropped lamb finds shelter from the wind.
And hither does one poet sometimes row
His pinnace . . . and beneath this roof
He makes his summer couch, and here at noon
Spreads out his limbs, while, yet unshorn, the sheep
Panting beneath the burthen of their wool
Lie round him, even as if they were a part
Of his own household: nor, while from his bed
He through that door-place looks toward the lake
And to the stirring breezes, does he want
Creations lovely as the work of sleep,
Fair sights, and visions of romantic joy.

William Wordsworth
(*"Lyrical Ballads, 1805"*)

The
ILLUSTRATED
LAKE POETS

MOLLY LEFEBURE

TIGER BOOKS INTERNATIONAL
LONDON

This edition published in 1992 by
Tiger Books International plc,
London

ISBN 1 85501 266 9

copyright © 1987 Toppan Printing Co Ltd

All rights reserved. No part of this book may be
reproduced or transmitted in any form or by any
means, electronic or mechanical, including
photocopying, recording or by any information
storage or retrieval system, without permission in
writing from the Publisher.

Printed in Singapore

CONTENTS

CHAPTER ONE

VISIONS OF ROMANTIC JOY

*T*he Picturesque Tourists, as the early visitors to the Lakes were known, had an absolute passion for peaks, for echoes, and for vapours, the Romantic name for mists and clouds. Peaks were, of course, an integral feature of the Lake Country, and vapours arose everywhere without prompting. As mists, they floated upward from the valleys, to become clouds encircling the mountain tops, or mysteriously enshrouding the landscape. The region, by its very nature, was equally productive of echoes, but natural echoes were not enough to satisfy the true enthusiast of the Romantic and the Picturesque. By the close of the eighteenth century the natural echoes of Ullswater had been supplemented by a barge equipped with small cannon which were fired for the gratification of tourists, producing salvoes of echoing and re-echoing sound. At other suitable spots french horns were placed. These, we are told, had "a very wonderful and pleasing effect".

The charge for echoes from cannon at Patterdale at the head of Ullswater was as follows (quoting from an invoice for the period):

To an echo, first quality	£0 10s 0
To do., second quality	£0 5s. 0

THE FIRST WAVE OF TOURISM

These early tourists belonged exclusively to what was known as "carriage trade": wealthy persons, touring the Lakes in their own carriages, accompanied by retinues of servants, and well able to afford what were then immensely high prices for echoes – many labourers supported a wife and children on five shillings a week. James Clarke, in his 1789 *Survey of the Lakes*, offered this advice to tourists, "If a traveller should have an opportunity . . . I would advise him to

take a fowling piece with him, to fire as a signal to his servant (who must remain in the valley) that he is above the mist; then the servant fire his piece, and the magnificent report will be a matter of great curiosity." It would have been a matter of even greater curiosity if the traveller had been touring the Lakes without a servant in attendance.

On October 27th 1799, however, there set off into the region of lakes, mountains, echoes and vapours, two somewhat shabbily dressed young men, travelling on foot, unaccompanied by servants

A GENTLEMAN IN A BOAT fires his fowling piece to produce echoes over Wastwater, a lake surrounded by mountains which (to quote Coleridge) "Are the Monsters of the Country, bare bleak Heads, evermore doing Deeds of Darkness, weather-plots, & storm-conspiracies in the clouds." This is one of Allom's most popular illustrations for Thomas Rose's "Westmorland, Cumberland, Durham and Northumberland", published 1832–1835.

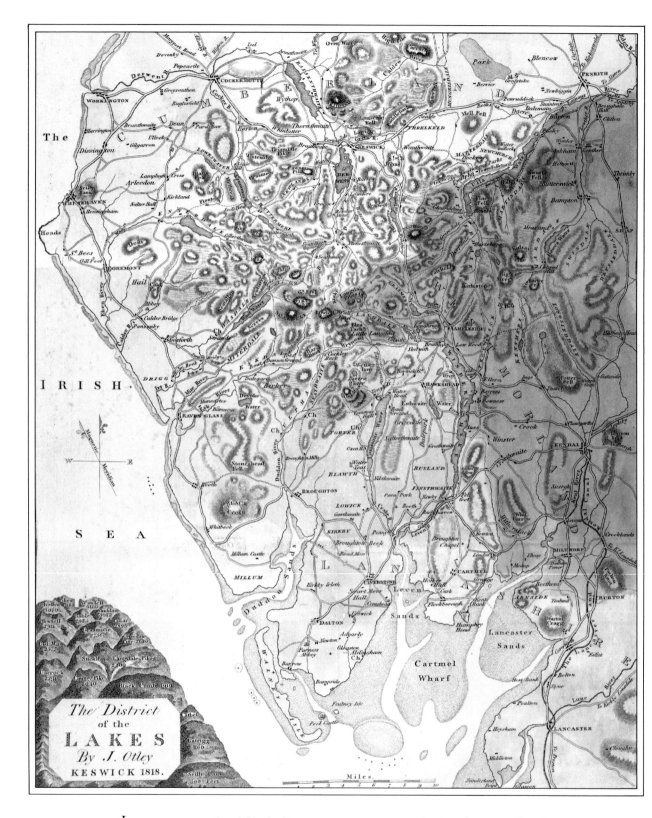

JONATHAN OTLEY produced this, the first accurate tourist map, in 1818, and it is still admirably reliable, if we remember that the three Lake Counties have now become one: Cumbria. Otley, a basket maker of ancient Grasmere stock, went to Keswick as a young man and took up residence in a quaint little cottage known as "Jonathan's Up the Steps" in King's Head Yard, where he lived for the rest of his life. He became a distinguished geologist, botanist and scientific observer, and was the host to many famous scientists.

and joking with one another about making a "pikteresk toor" of the Lakes. They were William Wordsworth and Samuel Taylor Coleridge: the latter with a considerable reputation as a poet; the former not as yet so well known. For some time past they had shared tentative plans to settle in the Lakes, there to live as close neighbours and partners in poetry, as they had been at Nether Stowey, Somersetshire, for twelve months from midsummer 1797. In that year they had produced the first edition of their joint work, *Lyrical Ballads*, and Coleridge had written much of his greatest and most exciting poetry, including *Frost at Midnight*, *Kubla Khan* and *The Rime of the Ancient Mariner*.

This wonderful year in Somerset had been followed by several months in Germany, Coleridge going there (without his wife and children) to study German at Ratzeburg and Goettingen, and Wordsworth and his sister Dorothy going with him, their announced intention being to learn German too. However, on arriving in Germany, brother and sister removed themselves to Goslar, where they spent the winter months alone together in deepest seclusion, learning no German, but with William absorbed in writing some of the finest poetry he had yet written. The Wordsworths had returned to England in April,

WALLERGILL FORCE, Coleridge's "silvery steep Water course", here seen with Haweswater lying below. A.G. Bradley in his "Highways and Byways in the Lake District" (1908) described it as "Among the most beautiful of northern waters: some three miles long and a bare half mile broad, in a trough of hills that rise in height as they near the lake head". Bradley went on to praise Mardale's "snug inn, the Dun Bull – and ancient church set among yew trees"; now all submerged in the vastly swollen Haweswater reservoir.

1799, while Coleridge remained in Germany for another three months. Meanwhile the Cumbrian born and bred Wordsworths, with a view to house-hunting in their native Lake Country, had travelled northwards, pausing to stay with childhood friends, the Hutchinsons, who farmed at Sockburn-on-Tees, in County Durham.

Here Coleridge, together with Joseph Cottle, the Bristolian publisher of *Lyrical Ballads*, had joined them at the end of October. There was much discussion about a second and enlarged edition of *Lyrical Ballads*, after which Cottle left for London, to talk business with publishers, and the poets headed for the hills. They were joined at Temple Sowerby by Wordsworth's sailor brother John, on shore leave between ships.

COLERIDGE'S INITIATION

The Lake Country was quite unknown to Devonshire-born Coleridge, though like everyone else of that day and age he had heard a great deal of its famed picturesque qualities, and the Wordsworths had given him much enticing first hand information about the region. Indeed it was the Wordsworths who, with their own infectious enthusiasm for the Lakes, had made him keen to go and live there. Now Wordsworth had arranged this pedestrian tour to introduce Coleridge to this most special and beautiful part of the world.

The first lake in Wordsworth's itinerary was Haweswater. At that time, no one would have dreamt that it was later to be flooded to make a reservoir for Manchester. This lake was considered by many to be the most beautiful in the region, with the little hamlet of Mardale reposing in the deep glen at its head, a gem of romantic loveliness and seclusion. Coleridge, who jotted his experiences and sensations in a notebook as he travelled, exclaimed over the dramatic contrasts discoverable in the landscape: "The simple & tame Beauty of encircled lower Lake, & the wild betongued savage mountained upper Lake"; the opposition of Waller Crag, "wooded up to the Top"; and the naked rocks of the "silvery steep Water course", to which he and his companion climbed.

From Mardale, they made their way by Nan Bield Pass and the old Garburn road to Troutbeck and from there to Windermere, where a view of the distant Langdale Pikes took Coleridge's breath away. "Huge ragged mountains, rising one above the other in wild relations of posture", he scribbled excitedly. By ferry across Windermere, to Esthwaite and Hawkshead, scenes of Wordsworth's happy schooldays (as unlike as might possibly be from Coleridge's far less happy boyhood spent at school in the heart of London, at

THE STARTLING VIEW of the Langdale Pikes that took Coleridge's breath away as he and his fellow walkers approached the head of Windermere and had their first sight of this celebrated rampart, guarding the upper end of Great Langdale.

IN WORDSWORTH'S YOUTH Hawkshead was an important market town for the leather goods and woollen industries; wool yarn was brought there from as far afield as Borrowdale, and saddlers and shoe-makers came from West Cumberland. The womenfolk were all engaged in spinning and weaving: even today the architecture of the little town bears witness to this industry. John Harden, who made this sketch of Hawkshead, moved with his wife and mother-in-law into Brathay Hall, near Windermere, in 1804 and soon built up a wide circle of friends, including the Wordsworths and Mrs. Coleridge and her children. His skilful sketches and watercolours not only vividly depict daily life at Brathay Hall, but the locality in general.

Christ's Hospital). The motherless nine-year-old William, together with his eleven-year-old brother Richard (sons of John Wordsworth, attorney, of Cockermouth) had entered Hawkshead grammar school at Whitsuntide, 1779. Later they had been joined by their brothers, John and Christopher.

While at the Grammar School, the Wordsworth boys lodged with Ann and Hugh Tyson, a childless couple who treated their young lodgers as if they had been their own brood. Ann Tyson had been in service at Rydal Mount before her marrige. Widowed in 1784, she had continued to take boarders until 1789, two years after William Wordsworth had left Hawkshead to become a Cambridge undergraduate. The summer before her retirement, Wordsworth had stayed with her during his Long Vacation and the proud old woman had paraded him around Hawkshead showing him off to her neighbours, some of whom had found it hard to recognize, in the rather dandyish youth, the schoolboy of yesteryear.

By the time Wordsworth brought Coleridge to Hawkshead, in the course of their 1799 walking tour, Ann Tyson had been three years in her grave. Wordsworth, showing Coleridge round the tiny market town, spoke long and lovingly of the simple old woman whom he and his brothers had "honoured with little less than filial love".

The visit to Hawkshead concluded, the three pedestrians moved on to Rydal and Grasmere, the beautiful little vale with its lake and single green island with which Wordsworth had fallen in love while still a schoolboy. Here, in the autumn rain of 1799, Wordsworth spotted "a small house" (Dove Cottage) standing empty and wrote to Dorothy that it might do for them to rent.

The weather was distinctly poor, but nevertheless

THE VILLAGE OF GRASMERE, much as Gray described it in 1769: "The bosom of the mountains, spreading here into a broad bason, discover in the midst Grasmere-water . . . from the shore, a low promontary pushes itself far into the water, and on it stands a white village, with a parish church rising in the midst of it: hanging inclosures, corn fields, the meadows, green as emerald, with their trees, and hedges and cattle, fill up the whole space from the edge of the water . . . above, a broken line of crags, that crown the scene . . . a little unsuspected Paradise.

an ascent was made of Helvellyn. From the summit, between clouds and mist, they had a panoramic view of "the Lake of Grasmere like a sullen Tarn . . . the luminous Cunneston Lake . . . Wyandermere with its Island . . . [and] the gloomy Ullswater", Coleridge wrote in his, by now damp, notebook. But, despite his jokes about "Pikteresk Toorists", Coleridge shared their enthusiasm for "vapours" and the wet weather could only breed more clouds and mist to delight him. His notebook jottings reveal his enchantment: "Exquisite Network of Film so instinct with gentle motion which, now the Shower only steadies, & now

it melts it into such a mistiness as the Breath leaves on a mirror –". And, a little later: "Mist as from a volcano", he wrote, as clouds surged up from the valley below.

John Wordsworth now left them and Wordsworth and Coleridge took the old turnpike road to Keswick, crossing Dunmail Raise, the county boundary between Westmorland and Cumberland. Their road led them past Thirlmere, a century later to have its level raised by over fifty feet, to form another reservoir for Manchester. This was to cause havoc in the traditional landscape and drown farmsteads and communities.

OLD THIRLMERE: the two adjoining lakes, Leathes Water (in the foreground) and Whythburn Water beyond, with the celtic bridge; Helvellyn soaring high on the left of the picture, its summit touched by cloud. The scene is bathed in Claudian sunset-glow. The wain and ponderous dray-horses (right foreground) are probably intended to carry an echo from "An Evening Walk", in which just such a wain and its team are described at the close of the day.

Thirlmere in those days consisted of two adjoining lakes, Wythburn Water and Leathes Water, connected near the centre by a narrow and shallow channel, between Dale Head Hall on the eastern shore and Armboth House (now submerged) on the west. This channel was crossed by a ford with stepping stones, and an ancient Celtic bridge. Coleridge, gazing up the Vale of St John, saw the glowering head of Saddleback topped with snow, black crags between the snow streaks. The wild scenery prompted him to political imagery: "That rude wrinkled beetling forehead of rock – all between on both sides savage & hopeless – obstinate Sansculottism", he mused.

At Keswick they heard talk of a house, intended for renting, that was soon to be built on a knoll overlooking the river Greta just outside the town. Discussing the possibilities of this as a future residence for Coleridge, the two men walked down the eastern shore of Bassenthwaite Lake and, after spending the night in the inn at Ouse Bridge, crossed Embleton Common to Lorton and from there continued to Crummock Water and Buttermere. Coleridge became increasingly excited as first Loweswater, then Crummock, and finally Buttermere came into view. He scribbled harder and faster in his notebook, he clambered up here, ran ahead there, all in order to obtain better views. "O God, what a scene!" he exclaimed as he had his first peep of

For the picturesque tourists of the 1790's and early nineteenth century the Lake Country scenery carried political nuances, as well as visions of Romantic joy. This view of St. John's in the Vale, with the snow-streaked Saddleback in the distance, is exactly that which prompted Coleridge to describe the scene as "savage and hopeless – obstinate Sansculottism": the Sansculottes being, at least in the public mind, the Paris mobs responsible for the worst excesses of the Revolutionary Terror in France; the dark aspects of Nature lurking behind the sunny foreground.

Crummock Water. At last: "Buttermere comes upon us, a fragment of it – the view enclosed by a huge Concave Semicircle – The Hill like a Dolphin so beautiful in the Lines of Snow in Crummock is named Red Pike – the Ridge that seems to run in behind it is named the High Stele – On our left where first we see the Buttermere is the Crag House Crags."

From Buttermere they visited Scale Force, a cascade with the highest unbroken vertical drop in the region. They crossed the boggy upland mosses of

CRAG HOUSES, to the right of the picture, the first habitations met by Wordsworth and Coleridge as they approached Buttermere, constituted most of this hamlet, apart from a mill, a farm or two and the Fish Inn – shown here with smoke coming from its chimney – home of Mary Robinson, the celebrated Beauty of Buttermere who, by 1799, was an established tourist attraction, thanks to Joseph Budworth who had first drawn attention to her charms in his "A Fortnight's Ramble to the Lakes" (1792). Her seduction by and bigamous marriage to a glamorous conman, John Hadfield, who was arrested on their "honeymoon" and hanged, elevated her to the status of true Romantic heroine.

black, now half hid by the mist, & ever & anon the waterfall in them flashing thro' the mists . . . a dark misty thunder-murmured Scene."

A SENSE OF ROMANCE

Wordsworth's route, following tracks and ancient roads and passes through the very heart of the district, known to none but the local people – shepherds and quarrymen, drovers and packmen – was essentially a route only to be devised by one who had been born and bred in the area and had roamed the hills as a boy. It was not a standard Picturesque Tourist's route, by any stretch of the imagination, but then the two young men were not conventional tourists.

However Wordsworth, had he chosen, could have conducted Coleridge on a traditional tour, showing him all the conventional scenes and sights. Wordsworth's youthful poem, *An Evening Walk* (written when he was eighteen, while at Cambridge, and published five years later, in 1793) was virtually an inventory of everything dear to the Picturesque Tourist's heart.

Floutern, slept the night at the foot of Ennerdale Broadwater, then next day went on to Wastwater and after a night in Wasdale Head crossed the Sty Head Pass to Borrowdale. Coleridge jotted a brief but wonderful word picture as they climbed out of Spouthead to gain the summit of the pass with Great Gable lowering on their left, the Scafells soaring in to the mists on their right, and the fellsides pouring with water after a night of heavy rain: "Brooks in their anger – all the Gullies full & white & the Chasms now

Far from my dearest friend, 'tis mine to rove
Thro' bare grey dell, high wood, and pastoral cove;
His wizard course where hoary Derwent takes
Thro' craggs, and forest glooms, and opening lakes,
Staying his silent waves, to hear the roar
That stuns the tremulous cliffs of high Lodore:
Where silver rocks the savage prospect chear
Of giant yews that frown on Rydale's mere;
Where peace to Grasmere's lonely island leads,
To willowy hedgerows, and to emerald meads;
Leads to her bridge, rude church, and cottag'd grounds,
Her rocky sheepwalks, and her woodland bounds;
Where bosom'd deep, the shy Winander peeps
'Mid clustering isles, and holly-sprinkl'd steeps;
Where twilight glens endear my Esthwaite's shore,
And memory of departed pleasures, more.

After this careful start, Wordsworth proceeded to pull out all the stops. Clouds, vapours, cascades, precipices, storm scenes, tinted autumn woods, flying sails on the bosom of a lake, peasants, panniered pack-trains, a slate quarry, dray-horses and timber wains, lonesome chapels, cattle browsing, shepherd boys waving their hats, Druid stones, apparitions and phantoms, humble cottages with smoke wreathing upward from their chimneys, pitiful vagrants, twinkling glow-worms, swains plodding homeward, swans on silver waters, sunset, twilight, moonlight, candles glimmering in cottage windows, the song of unseen mountain streams in the darkness. A poet roaming and dreaming.

It was through this poem that Wordsworth and Coleridge had first become acquainted. Coleridge, two years Wordsworth's junior, had been in his final year at Cambridge when he had read the poem and had been deeply and immediately impressed. "Seldom, if ever, was the emergence of an original poetic genius above the literary horizon more evidently announced," he had declared. Fired by his enthusiasm he had written to Wordsworth, with the result that some time in September 1795 the two had met in Bristol.

It was Wordsworth's imagery in *An Evening Walk* that awakened Coleridge's initial interest in the Lake Country.

"... *mid the calm of summer nights*
When by the margin of the trembling lake
Beneath the gloomy hills I homeward went
In solitude ..."
William Wordsworth: "The Prelude" (1798–1799)

— Then Quiet led me up the huddling rill,
Bright'ning with water-breaks the sombrous gill;
To where, while thick above the branches close,
In dark-brown bason its wild waves, repose,
Inverted shrubs, and moss of darkest green,
Cling from the rocks, with pale wood-weeds between;
Save that, atop, the subtle sunbeams shine,
On wither'd briars that o'er the craggs recline;
Sole light admitted here, a small cascade,
Illumes with sparkling foam the twilight shade,
Beyond, along the vista of the brook,
Where antique roots its bustling path o'erlook,
The eye reposes on a secret bridge
Half grey, half shagg'd with ivy to its ridge.

— Sweet rill, farewell! Tomorrow's noon again,
Shall hide me wooing long thy wildwood strain;
But now the sun has gain'd his western road,
And eve's mild hour invites my steps abroad . . .

I love to mark the quarry's moving trains,
Dwarf pannier'd steeds, and men, and numerous wains:
How busy the enormous hive within,
While Echo dallies with the various din!
Some hardly heard their chissel's clinking sound,
Toil, small as pigmies, in the gulph profound;
Some, dim between th'aëreal cliffs descry'd,

O'erwalk the viewless plank from side to side;
These by the pale-blue rocks that ceaseless ring
Glad from their airy baskets hang and sing . . .

I love beside the glowing lake to stray,
Where winds the road along the secret bay . . .
Along the "wild meand'ring" shore to view,
Obsequious Grace the winding swan pursue . . .
Stately, and burning in his pride, divides
And glorying looks around, the silent tides:
On as he floats, the silver'd waters glow,
Proud of the varying arch and moveless form of snow . . .

The song of mountain streams unheard by day,
Now hardly heard, beguiles my homeward way.
All air is, as the sleeping water, still,
List'ning th'aëreal music of the hill,
Broke only by the slow clock tolling deep,
Or shout that wakes the ferry-man from sleep,
Soon follow'd by his hollow-parting oar,
And echo'd hoof approaching the far shore;
Sound of clos'd gate, across the water born,
Hurrying the feeding hare thro' rustling corn;
The tremulous sob of the complaining owl;
And at long intervals the mill-dog's howl;
The distant forge's swinging thump profound;
Or yell in the deep woods of lonely hound.

THE DAWN OF CHANGE

It seems hard to believe that a mere forty years previously there had been no Picturesque Lake Country. Nobody had come to the Lakes of northern England in search of clouds, vapours and echoes, and anyone speaking of going there to seek for these things would have been laughed at. Hard-headed business men traditionally journeyed to Cumberland, Westmorland and Lancashire-North-of-the-Sands (the three counties which now make up Cumbria) for wool and textiles, pig iron and plumbago, coal and slate, charcoal, bobbins and brushes. This region, with its pits and mines and quarries, foundries and mills, was one of the largest and busiest, as well as one of the most ancient industrial regions in Britain: but as for clouds, peaks and vapours, these were, literally speaking, strictly for the birds.

The inaccessibility of the region by road was notorious. Industry depended upon the thriving sea ports of west Cumberland, from which ships sailed to all parts of the world, as well as to the home ports of Liverpool and London. It took fourteen days to reach London from Kendal by road. However, from 1750 onwards, there was a rapid development of turnpike roads and access to the region by road improved immeasurably. These improvements, together with the latest cultural phenomenon, opened up the mountainous and misty north to a wholly new kind of industry: Romantic and Picturesque Tourism.

Romantic sensibility (by which taste was guided so closely that taste and sensibility became inextricably welded), owed to Jean-Jacques Rousseau its paramount insistence upon the natural, the wild, the primitive and the instinctive. The Noble Savage was his dominant theme – the unspoilt Child of Nature.

"How busy the enormous hive within,
While Echo dallies with the various din!"

The industrious labour of the local men in the gothic caverns of the northern quarries and mines was considered highly Romantic by the Picturesque School, hence the reason for the description of a quarry in Wordsworth's "An Evening Walk". This meticulously observed quarry scene by Thomas Allom gives us a fascinatingly detailed glimpse of what slate quarrying was like in the early nineteenth century. It was a very important industry for the region in those days.

THIS 1795 ENGRAVING BY MERIGOT from a drawing by John "Warwick" Smith epitomizes the sublime delights of solitary evening roaming. The two anglers, caught by the western sky's sunset glow reflected from the motionless lake, emphasize the lonely grandeur of the scene. The shadow of Nab Scar, on thee right, is creeping gradually across Rydal Water; Silver Howe, in the background, shines in the lingering gleams of last sunlight. Gray's "Elegy" steals upon the mind:

"Now fades the glimmering landscape on the sight,
And all the air a solemn stillness holds."

Within every man of taste and refinement there lurked a noble savage, or such, at any rate, was the impression that all men of taste and refinement hoped to give. Every cultivated young lady saw herself as a sportive child of Nature.

The evening walk, so fashionable with these people, equally owed its popularity to Rousseau. His *Rêveries du Promeneur Solitaire* first taught western man to appreciate a country stroll, above all when taken in the evening. From this solitary ramble of Rousseau's, many developments were to spring.

The kind of scenery admired by fashionable evening strollers came to be associated with certain favourite pictures. Thus the scenery was termed "Picturesque", paintings and landscape together becoming intertwined in the movement we now know as the Picturesque School. Thence the fashion

entered a fugual stage, whereby enthusiasts sought scenery that was considered suitable for the painting which they so much admired.

The three painters most esteemed by lovers of the Picturesque were Claude Lorrain (known simply as Claude), Nicolas Poussin and Salvator Rosa. Their scenery abounded in dramatic mountain peaks, rivers and winding lakes, skies filled with clouds, all bathed in an out-of-this-world sunset glow – the famous glow introduced by Claude. Thomas Smith, ("Smith of Derby"), first drew full attention to the Picturesque quality of the English Lakes. He knew the region and realised that its landscape was of the sort that was becoming so fashionable. Full of enterprise, he took himself off on a sketching expedition and his resultant engravings of Derwent Water, Windermere and Thirlmere, published in 1761, were an instant

success. In 1767, they were re-published by popular demand, together with a fourth view: Ennerdale Broadwater. However, by far the most successful of these four views was that of Derwent Water, taken from Crow Park, Keswick, subsequently to become one of the most celebrated viewpoints in the entire Lake Country.

The Picturesque *cognoscente* responded to Smith's *View of Derwent Water* with effusive praise, not for Smith's artistry but for the view itself: "The full perfection of Keswick consists of three circumstances, beauty, horror and immensity united – to give you a complete idea of these three perfections, would require the united powers of Claude, Salvator and Poussin", enthused one connoisseur (John Brown, of St. John's College, Cambridge).

Note the use of the word "immensity", linked with the adjectives "horrible", "terrible" and "dreadful". We are, in fact, face to face with the Sublime. "Sublime" is not a word much used today, but it was a hugely popular adjective with the Picturesque School. The source of English thinking on this subject was Burke's *Philosophical Inquiry into the Origin of our Ideas on the Sublime and Beautiful*, first published in 1756. The Sublime, said Burke, should arouse apprehensions of the grand, the noble, the overwhelming;

"THE ENCHANTED CASTLE" by Claude Lorrain (1600–82), the Old Master whose work most inspired the Romantic School. Jonathan Richardson, the critic whose essays, for the best part of a century, guided the taste of cultivated persons in Britain, wrote in 1722: 'Of all the Landskip-Painters, Claude Lorrain has the most Beautiful and Pleasing Ideas." Turner extolled Claude as: "Pure as Italian air, calm, beautiful and serene . . . Replete with . . . comprehensive qualities and powers." This painting, originally called "Psyche Outside the Palace of Cupid", is probably his most famous.

The Rev. John Dalton of Queen's College, Oxford, burst into verse on the subject of what he called *Agreeable Sensations derived from the Horror of Falling Rocks*:

> Channels by rocky torrents torn
> Rocks to the lakes in thunders borne,
> O'er such as o'er our heads appear
> Suspended in their mid career . . .
> I view with wonder and delight
> A pleasant, though an awful sight.

Even Coleridge proved to be subject to this kind of imaginative terror. When he visited Scale Force he was fascinated not so much by the idea of having rocks fall upon him, as by the notion of falling himself. He wrote in his notebook: "The first fall a stupendous Height . . . The chasm thro' which it flows is stupendous – so wildly wooded that the mosses & wet weeds & perilous Tree increase the Horror of the rocks which *ledge* only enough to interrupt not stop your fall – & the Tree – O God! to think of a poor Wretch hanging with one arm from it!".

There was no reason why anyone should ever find themselves hanging by one arm from this tree, but it was a pleasing thought.

All this made a tour of the Lakes immeasurably more exciting for the Picturesque Tourist than it might otherwise have been. Falling boulders, which did not actually come whizzing through the air to knock one on the head, but which definitely had the potential to do so; mists, in which the unwary might be lost and perish horribly, only one took great care not to go up into the mists; and torrents, which might bear the unheeding away in the twinkling of an eye. Lovers of the Sublime also brooded on the terror of tripping over precipices, falling into chasms, being sucked into peat bogs – there really was no end to the thrillingly horrible things that could happen to a tourist in the Lake Country! Fortunately, one made

he went on to stress that, in mountain scenery, there should always be an element of fear, but that this must terminate in repose.

This famous definition of the Sublime was to be, in turn, defined by the Picturesque Tourists as "The art of becoming horribly alarmed without having to entertain serious fears for one's personal safety." From this popular demand for thrills without spills, the intelligensia evolved an aesthetic theory of the Horrid and Terrible, which prompted Aiken's essay on *The Pleasure Derived from Objects of Terror and the Enquiry into Those Kinds of Distress which Excite Agreeable Sensations.*

the tour of the Lakes in one's carriage, and if one did venture up a mountain it was *never* without a guide. But for the unfortunate, or the unwary – oh, dreadful to contemplate!

SEDUCTION OF A POET

In 1769, lured by Thomas Smith's view, there had come to Keswick the first true poet to be tempted to the Lakes: Thomas Gray, author of the famous *Elegy Written in a Country Churchyard*, a poem directly inspired by Rousseau's *Rêveries* and itself the inspiration behind Wordsworth's *An Evening Walk*. It would be safe to say that Gray's *Elegy* was the most popular, as well as possibly the most influential, poem of its era.

Gray, while at Keswick, spent much time strolling on the shores of Derwent Water, admiring the celebrated view. He also ventured part of the way up Borrowdale, as far as the little hamlet of Grange. He found it a terrifying journey, along a boulder-strewn road deep into the mountains; he was convinced that danger lurked around every corner. Happily, nothing dreadful actually occurred. No rocks fell on him from the cliffs overhanging the road, and all the natives he

encountered proved courteous and friendly – although desperate men, he was solemnly assured, lurked in the distant hills. It is impossible to resist the suspicion that Gray was having his leg pulled! During his strolls in Crow Park and Borrowdale, Gray was constantly stopping to write notes in his journal, or to admire a view in the approved manner of the day,

---

VERSES FROM ELEGY

Written in a Country Churchyard

I

The curfew tolls the knell of parting day,
The lowing herds wind slowly o'er the lea,
The ploughman homeward plods his weary way,
And leaves the world to darkness and to me.

II

Now fades the glimmering landscape on the sight,
And all the air a solemn stillness holds,
Save where the beetle wheels his droning flight,
And drowsy tinklings lull the distant folds;

III

Save that from yonder ivy-mantled tower,
The moping owl does to the moon complain
Of such, as wandering near her secret bower,
Molest her ancient solitary reign.

IV

Beneath those rugged elms, that yew-tree's shade,
Where heaves the turf in many a mould'ring heap,
Each in his narrow cell for ever laid,
The rude forefathers of the hamlet sleep.

Thomas Gray

"*Derwentwater from Crow Park*" *by Thomas Smith, looking up towards the so-called Jaws of Borrowdale, with little Castle Crag in the centre, and Lodore Cascade clearly visible to the left. The scene abounds with various Picturesque and Sublime features: Pocklington's island and the smaller St. Herbert's Isle; details such as the plume of smoke rising from the cottage chimneys, and little boats on "the bosom of the lake"; the green fields and groves of the eastern shore; the rocks, cliffs and shaggily wooded steeps of the western shore; the vapours; the lofty mountains in the distance, piercing the clouds: "Beauty, horror, and immensity united."*

which was to stand with one's back to the view and to gaze at its reflection in a Claude-glass, an essential item of a Picturesque Tourist's equipment. The Claude-glass was, basically, a plano-convex mirror some four inches in diameter (two glasses were in fact recommended, and indeed usually carried, bound up like a pocket book). One mirror was dark, on black foil, for use in sunshine, while the other was backed with silver foil, for use on dark and gloomy days, and was usually tinted to give the classical "golden glow" of Claude's canvasses. The virtues of the glass were advertised thus: "Where the objects are great and near, it removes them to a due distance, and shows them in the soft colours of nature, and in the most regular perspective the eye can perceive, or science demonstrate."

Gray made his first visit in October, in order to receive the fullest possible measure of autumnal mists and vapours. He was not disappointed; the changeability of the weather and of the skyscape fulfilled all his poetic expectations. As he walked in Crow Park a "little shower fell, red clouds came marching up the hills from the east, and part of a bright rainbow seemed to rise along the side of Castle Hill". He took his evening strolls: "The clouds came rolling up the mountains all round, very dark, yet the moon shone at intervals".

In sum, Gray must be seen as the prototype of all the Picturesque Tourists who were to follow; equipped with notebook and Claude-glass and afire with Romantic enthusiasm, yet simultaneously deliciously chilled by *frissons* of the Sublime.

THE TAMING OF A LANDSCAPE

Gradually a number of approved viewpoints became established as spots where tourists of taste and sensibility stationed themselves, back to the view, Claude-glass in hand, to revel in the scene. Thus these viewpoints came to be known as "stations". Increasingly the visitor was advised how to look at landscape, how to judge what was seen. In 1786 there appeared William Gilpin's *Observations on . . . the Mountains and Lakes of Cumberland and Westmorland relative chiefly to Picturesque Beauty*. This work laid down the most categorical "picturesque rules".

Nature, as Gilpin himself confessed, did not always conform with the Gilpin taste. Nothing dismayed by this, Gilpin, in his sketches, did not hesitate to rectify Nature's errors, admitting artlessly, "I am so attached to my picturesque rules, that if nature goes wrong I cannot help putting her right."

Gainsborough, who visited the Lakes in the summer of 1783, was a fascinating example of a painter who adapted nature to accord with his ideas of the picturesque. Reynolds has left us an account of how Gainsborough built model landscapes on his

THE FAMOUS DOUBLE-SPAN PACK-HORSE BRIDGE at Grange, near which Thomas Gray met "a civil young farmer" who insisted on conducting Gray across the bridge and into "a neat white house in the village" where he was given refreshment and topographical information. The house is still there; the River Derwent still flows, as Gray described it, "Clear as glass, and showing . . . every trout that passes."

THOMAS GAINSBOROUGH, essentially Metropolitan Man, a fashionable portrait painter and sophisticate of Bath and London, dreamed, predictably, of Arcady: "I wish very much to walk off to some sweet Village where I can paint Landskips." In 1782, he visited Cumberland and Westmorland, announcing his intention to expose "your Grays and Dr Brownes" as mere "tawdry fan Painters" and on his return to London "to mount all the Lakes, at the next Exhibition, in the great stile". Here is a Borrowdale scene depicted "in the great stile"; not recognizably Borrowdale, but immensely Picturesque.

studio table, in preference to going into the country to look at the real thing. He composed candle-lit rustic scenes using broken stones, cork and coal and broccoli, and pieces of looking-glass, which he magnified and improved into rocks, trees and water. He also made little models of peasants, cows, waggons and horses, finding these models more pleasingly picturesque than the real thing. Country

life in the raw can at times be a little squalid.

Despite the fact that today we associate the Lakes predominantly with poets, it was in fact the painters, rather than poets, who were attracted to the region during these years of early tourism. They were not all tempted to "put Nature right", like Gilpin, or "construct" scenes as Gainsborough did (and as Constable, too, was occasionally tempted to do). In 1777 and 1778 Sir George Beaumont, a rich patron of the arts and himself an amateur painter of considerable talent, visited the Lakes on sketching tours. His companions were Thomas Hearne, the engraver, and Joseph Farington, the last of whom, especially, has left a series of remarkable portrayals of the Lake Country that he saw, rather than views which he felt he should have seen.

Turner made his first tour of the north of England, including the Lake Country, in 1797. He returned there in 1801 on his way home from his first Scottish tour. Francis Towne was there in 1786, while Loutherbourg had been there in 1783 (possibly in the company of Gainsborough). John Crome was in Keswick in 1802; John Glover had made his first visit by 1795; and Constable came to the Lakes in 1806.

"CROSSING THE SANDS", from Lancaster over Morecambe Bay at low tide, was an historic route: in medieval times, the monks of Cartmel Priory were responsible for providing guides, later this responsibility passed to the duchy of Lancaster. Crossing without a guide was dangerous because of the treacherous estuary tides. Nevertheless, the route was popular with the Picturesque Tourists, encouraged by West's assurance that, "With the proper guides, crossing the sands is a journey of little more danger than any other." Wordsworth also recommended it as the best introductory approach to the mountains; seen in all their grandeur as one travelled towards them across Morecambe Bay.

A TRADITION DEVELOPS

In 1778 there had appeared Thomas West's *Guide to the Lakes*, a "practical guide" as distinct from books dedicated to fashionably tasteful appreciation. West died in 1779, two months before the appearance of the second edition of his *Guide* and therefore he never knew the full extent of the success of the book, which by 1821 had gone into a further nine editions. A large measure of its success was undoubtedly due to its down-to-earth approach, "To describe every picturesque view that this region of landscape presents would be an endless labour; . . . The province of the Guide is to point out the stations, and leave to the company the enjoyment of reflection . . . This Guide shall therefore take up the company at Penrith and attend them on a tour to all the lakes; and to conducting the party from station to station, viewpoint to viewpoint."

This, of course, saved tourists a tremendous amount of time and trouble. West's stations became a ritualistic progress round the Lakes and many visitors did not linger to look at anything between these stipulated places.

By this time a regular coach service had commenced between London and Carlisle. The journey took about thirty six hours and doctors warned against such dangerous speeds of travel. More and more visitors appeared in the Lake Country. The rich began to build elegant Picturesque residences there, not infrequently permitting their personal Romantic fantasies to run riot, particularly in the embellishment of their grounds and outbuildings.

Outstanding in this field was Mr. Joseph Pocklington (nicknamed Lord Pocky by the Keswickians) a rich banker from the Midlands. Even before he came to the Lakes he was building all kinds of Picturesque extravaganzas. His Nottinghamshire

LANCASTER, river port and country town of Lancashire, is dominated by a Norman Castle and fine church, standing in an elevated position at the head of the Lune estuary. The city has a colourful history; sacked by Robert Bruce; restored, to become a stronghold of John of Gaunt; captured by Cromwell's troops in the Civil Wars; and marched through by Bonnie Prince Charlie in 1745. Less romantically, by the late eighteenth century, Lancaster clattered with cotton mills: from its riverside warehouses cotton goods were shipped to the Liverpool slavers who carried these cargoes to Africa, exchanging them for negroes, took the slaves across the Atlantic and returned to England with bales of raw cotton, grown by slaves clad in Lancashire cotton stuffs. A highly lucrative trade cycle! Lancaster was historically on the route to the Lake Counties and the Picturesque Tourists maintained this tradition; dwelling on the history of the city as they passed through, rather than the cotton and "the horrid trade of selling negroes".

estate records speak of oriental-style stables, obelisks galore, and (particularly pleasant) an "ornamental hovel". In 1778 he began building a house on Vicar's Isle, Derwent Water, soon to be known as "Pocklington's Isle". The basic cost of this house – excluding the more fanciful items of furniture and fittings – was £1,395, a lavish sum in those days. He embellished the island itself with his favourite obelisks, including one or two experimental samples created by lopping and carving oak trees to an obelisk shape which, painted white, achieved what he proudly described as "a ghastly effect" (ghastliness, in the sense of the horrible, being of course an aspect of the Sublime). He also built a Druid's Temple on the island, and a bang-up-to-date artillery battery, for procuring echoes.

In 1787, he built himself a new home in Borrowdale, naming it Barrow Cascade House – he built the cascade too, as a rival to the neighbouring Lodore Falls. He also erected many more obelisks, and a hermitage. He owned the land on which stood the celebrated Bowder Stone, an enormous fragment of rock, weighing an estimated 1,771 tons and 13 hundredweight (measured and estimated by Lord Pocky himself), which at some time in the distant past had broken away from the cliffs above. Close by the Bowder Stone, Pocklington built a small Gothic chapel, a "Druid monolith", and a small hermitage in which, during the season, he installed an ancient crone hired to represent a female recluse.

One might be tempted to ask what Keswick and Borrowdale had done to deserve all this. The answer was, that here, in this particular part of the district, the Picturesque School had discovered "beauty, horror and immensity united [to] full perfection".

And it was for this reason that the youthful Wordsworth, in the spirit of the Picturesque, had felt obliged to open *An Evening Walk* on the banks of "hoary Derwent" and among the "cliffs of high Lodore", rather than in the region of Grasmere or Rydale, places far nearer his heart than either Borrowdale or Keswick.

Looking north from the foot of the fabled Lake Windermere, with Fell Foot, the artist Mary Dixon's "elegant rustic residence".

*T*HE BOWDER STONE *rests upon a base surprisingly narrow, considering the Stone's enormous bulk. Pocklington had a small hole cut through the base and the old woman whom he hired as a "female recluse", during the tourist season, entertained visitors by shaking hands with them through this chink – the visitor lying down on one side of the Stone and the old woman on the other. The Sublimity of the thing was that the Stone might topple over at any moment and crush the visitor as he or she lay shaking hands! Pocklington's "gothic chapel" was modified into a cottage residence (shown here) for the old woman. Tourists, after shaking hands, were taken into the cottage to have a glass of lemonade and sign a visitors' book.*

CHANGING PERCEPTIONS

On Friday, November 15th, he and Coleridge walked down Borrowdale, laughing and joking together at the worst excesses of Lord Pocky. They stopped to inspect Lodore Falls, traditionally considered by the Picturesque School to be the most sublime sight of any in the Lakes, and described by Gilpin in these glowing terms: "The stream [of Watendlath] falls through a chasm between two towering perpendicular rocks. The intermediate part broken into large fragments, forms the rough bed of the cascade . . . Among these broken rocks the stream finds its way, through a fall of at least a hundred feet . . . Rocks and water in opposition can hardly produce a more animated strife. The ground at the bottom also is very

THERE WAS AN HOTEL at the foot of Lodore Falls as early as 1784. In this scene, a party of tourists, possibly staying at the hotel, are seen embarking in a rowing boat on Derwent Water; behind them the Lodore cascade plunges magnificently between the crags.

THE WHITE-PAINTED STONES of Castle Rigg are shown here by moonlight, with Helvellyn looming in the distance – the embodiment of a perfect Picturesque scene and a favourite tourist attraction in the late eighteenth century.

much broken, and overgrown with trees and thickets, amongst which the water is swallowed up into an abyss, and at length finds its way through deep channels to the lake."

The drawback with Lodore was, and still is, that it is only sublime at times of heavy rain; at other times it shrivels sadly. Indeed a tale is told of a tourist who asked where he might find Lodore Cascade, only to be told that he was sitting on it! Coleridge has so little to say of Lodore on this first occasion of visiting it that we are left with the feeling that November 15th, 1799 was a poor day for Lodore.

The two then went on to the stone circle of Castle Rigg, in that period always referred to as a Druid Temple. In order to give the stones a moonlit, ghastly, sublime effect they had been painted white. This stroke of the Picturesque enchanted the majority of tourists, but disgusted Wordsworth and Coleridge, who commented wrily: "The Keswickians have been playing Tricks with the stones".

The final lap of the pedestrian tour had now been reached. The poets trudged, just a little weary by now, across Threlkeld and Matterdale Commons, the Ullswater fells rising before them on the skyline.

Their final destination was Eusemere and the house of Thomas Clarkson, the abolitionist and a friend of Wordsworth's. Here Coleridge left Wordsworth and headed for London. Both he and Wordsworth would soon return to settle in the Lakes and in due course would radically change the way in which people looked at the scenery and felt and thought about the Lake Country.

THE VIEW that greeted Wordsworth and Coleridge on the final lap of their walk from Keswick, over Matterdale Common towards Ullswater.

CHAPTER TWO
"SEEING INTO THE LIFE OF THINGS"

*B*arely two months after Wordsworth had first found Dove Cottage standing empty, in Grasmere, he and his sister Dorothy had become tenants and had moved in, on Friday December 20th, 1799. They had travelled the greater part of their journey from Sockburn to Kendal (the county town of Westmorland) on foot, the wind at their backs bowling them along. At Kendal they ordered and bought furniture and then hired a post-chaise, in which they completed their journey to Grasmere, arriving there as the winter darkness closed in following a beautiful sunset. A deep excitement seized them:

> Bright and solemn was the sky
> That faced us with a passionate welcoming
> And led us to our threshold, to a home
> Within a home, what was to be, and soon,
> Our love within a love.
>
> *"Home at Grasmere"*

A neighbour, old Molly Fisher, had done her best to make the cottage dry and comfortable for their arrival, but despite her efforts the place, during their first months of residence, was damp and draughty. Both William and Dorothy caught troublesome colds.

For two months ceaseless winter storms raged outside while within the cottage Dorothy sat sewing for hours on end, "absolutely buried" by yards of cloth with which she was making curtains and bed hangings. Meantime Molly Fisher, who had been engaged to help with households chores, kept Dorothy entertained with stories about the neighbours.

The Grasmere of 1799 was little changed from the Grasmere which had enchanted Thomas Gray when he had visited it some thirty years earlier during the course of his tour of the Lakes. He had described it as "A little unsuspected *Paradise*." Nor were the villagers themselves much different from the un-

affected, kindly folk Wordsworth remembered from his boyhood; they were eager to be neighbourly and to help the newcomers settle in. There was certainly a great deal to be done. "We have been overhead in confusion, painting the rooms, mending the doors, and heaven knows what!" Wordsworth wrote to Coleridge at the end of the first week at Dove Cottage.

A DREAM BECOMES REALITY

But though a frenziedly busy time, it was also a very happy one for the brother and sister who had long dreamed of setting up home together in the Lakes.

A VIEW OF TOWNEND in Grasmere, as it was when the Wordsworths lived there. Dove Cottage can be seen on the right, slightly obscured by the tree. This "main road", leading out of Grasmere to Rydal and Ambleside, passed right by the cottage and here a horsedrawn cartload of hay is ambling along. The mighty Helm Crag can be seen rising up in the are background; Grasmere church and the lake itself out of view, hidden by the buildings on the left of the picture.

HAWKSHEAD FREE GRAMMAR SCHOOL, founded in 1585 by Edwin Sandys, Archbishop of York, though small in size, in its day enjoyed a good reputation as a seat of education. The school was rebuilt in 1675, and modernized in 1891, so the building we see today is not exactly as it was in Wordsworth's day.

As young children at Cockermouth they had been close companions. Dorothy was the only girl in the family, "a little prattler among men", as Wordsworth puts it in his poem *The Sparrow's Nest*, in which he recaptures an episode in their childhood.

Dorothy was only seven years old when her mother died, and she was sent to Halifax to be cared for by a relative, while the Wordsworth boys went away to school at Hawkshead. Within five years their father had died and the family remained scattered. At Halifax little Dorothy had lived happily with her aunt, while at Hawkshead William had revelled and rejoiced in the carefree life of a boy growing up among lakes and mountains. Following the separation of sister and brothers in the wake of family disaster, they were not reunited until a space of nine years had elapsed. William was then seventeen, Dorothy sixteen. They discovered that they shared a remarkable natural sympathy. During the next few years William went to Cambridge, and Dorothy went to live in Norfolk with her clergyman uncle William Cookson and his wife. But it was as if there had always been a special destination that would reunite brother and sister. Some mysterious force had drawn the exploring schoolboy to the little vale of Grasmere, with which he had instantly fallen in love and to which years later he, together with Dorothy, had joyfully returned.

THE SPARROW'S NEST

Behold, within the leafy shade,
Those bright blue eggs together laid!
On me the chance-discovered sight
Gleamed like a vision of delight.
I started – seeming to espy
The home and sheltered bed,
The Sparrow's dwelling, which, hard by
My Father's house, in wet or dry
My sister Emmeline and I
    Together visited.

She looked at it and seemed to fear it;
Dreading, tho' wishing, to be near it:
Such heart was in her, being then
A little Prattler among men.
The Blessing of my later years
Was with me when a boy:
She gave me eyes, she gave me ears;
And humble cares, and delicate fears;
A heart, the fountain of sweet tears;
    And love, and thought, and joy.

William Wordsworth

HOME AT GRASMERE

Embrace me then, ye Hills, and close me in;
Now in the clear and open day I feel
Your guardianship; I take it to my heart;
'Tis like the solemn shelter of the night.
But I would call thee beautiful, for mild,
And soft, and gay, and beautiful thou art
Dear Valley, having in thy face a smile
Though peaceful, full of gladness. Thou art pleased,
Pleased with thy crags and woody steeps, thy Lake,
Its one green island and its winding shores;
The multitude of little rocky hills,
Thy Church and cottages of mountain stone
Clustered like stars some few, but single most,
And lurking dimly in their shy retreats,
Or glancing at each other cheerful looks
Like separated stars with clouds between.
What want we? have we not perpetual streams,
Warm woods, and sunny hills, and fresh green fields,
And mountains not less green, and flocks and herds,
And thickets full of songsters, and the voice
Of lordly birds, an unexpected sound
Heard now and then from morn to latest eve,
Admonishing the man who walks below
Of solitude and silence in the sky?
These have we, and a thousand nooks of earth
Have also these, but nowhere else is found,
Nowhere (or is it fancy?) can be found
The one sensation that is here; 'tis here,
Here as it found its way into my heart
In childhood, here as it abides by day,
By night, here only; or in chosen minds

That take it with them hence, wher'er they go.
— 'Tis, (but I cannot name it) 'tis the sense
Of majesty, and beauty, and repose,
A blended holiness of earth and sky,
Something that makes this individual spot,
This small abiding-place of many men,
A termination, and a last retreat,
A centre, come from wheresoe'er you will,
A Whole without dependence or defect,
Made for itself, and happy in itself,
Perfect Contentment, Unity entire.
    Bleak season was it, turbulent and bleak,
When hitherward we journeyed side by side
Through burst of sunshine and through flying showers;
Paced the long Vales — how long they were — and yet
How fast that length of way was left behind,
Wensley's rich Vale, and Sedbergh's naked heights.
The frosty wind, as if to make amends
For its keen breath, was aiding to our steps,
And drove us onward like two ships at sea,
Or like two birds, companions in mid-air,
Parted and reunited by the blast.
    Stern was the face of nature; we rejoiced
In that stern countenance, for our souls thence drew
A feeling of their strength. The naked trees,
The icy brooks, as on we passed, appeared
To question us. 'Whence come ye, to what end?'
They seemed to say. 'What would ye?' said the shower,
'Wild Wanderers, whither through my dark domain?'
The sunbeam said, 'Be happy.'

William Wordsworth

ESTHWAITE WATER as it was in Wordsworth's youth. In winter, Wordsworth skated on this sylvan little lake, and in summer he roamed its shores in the early morning and at twilight.

THE ILLUSTRATED LAKE POETS

'THERE WAS A BOY'

There was a boy, ye knew him well, ye cliffs
And islands of Winander! Many a time,
At evening, when the stars had just begun
To move along the edges of the hills,
Rising or setting, would he stand alone,
Beneath the trees, or by the glimmering lake;
And there, with fingers interwoven, both hands
Pressed closely palm to palm and to his mouth
Uplifted, he, as through an instrument,
Blew mimic hootings to the silent owls
That they might answer him. And they would shout
Across the watery vale, and shout again
Responsive to his call, with quivering peals,
And long halloos, and screams, and echoes loud
Redoubled and redoubled; concourse wild
Of mirth and jocund din! And, when it chanced
That pauses of deep silence mocked his skill,
Then, sometimes, in that silence, while he hung
Listening, a gentle shock of mild surprise
Has carried far into his heart the voice
Of mountain torrents; or the visible scene
Would enter unawares into his mind
With all its solemn imagery, its rocks,
Its woods, and that uncertain heaven, received
Into the bosom of the steady lake.

William Wordsworth

A WANDERING YOUTH

Wordsworth came down from Cambridge in the summer of 1790 without having sat for his degree. He had only the vaguest ideas of how he might earn a living and before taking any hard decisions he set off on a walking tour in France. His guardians (uncles Richard Wordsworth and Christopher Crackenthorp) were dour with him on his return, asking him uncomfortable questions about what he, virtually a penniless young man, intended to do with his life? Finally Wordsworth decided to return to France to become proficient in the French language with a view to perhaps becoming travelling tutor to some young gentleman.

France was in the early throes of revolution and Wordsworth sympathized with the Revolution's ideals. For the next twelve months, living upon a frugal allowance from his uncles, he stayed in Paris, Orleans, and Blois. In Orleans, early in 1792, Wordsworth met and fell in love with a young woman named Annette Vallon, who came from a middle class, strongly Roman Catholic family in Blois. Although devout and convent reared, Annette, like so many girls of her generation, was aglow with Romanticism; fervent, ardent, a spontaneous "Child of Nature". The very air of France was at that time incandescent with Liberty and Freedom. Annette was staying in Orleans, far from family supervision, and before long she was pregnant by Wordsworth.

Annette never married her "Cher Villiams" (as she called him). It is sometimes suggested that the outbreak of war between France and England in 1793 prevented the marriage, but the much more likely explanation is that Annette's family refused to countenance the match. They were French Catholics; Wordsworth was a Protestant Englishman with exactly the kind of morals, or rather the lack of them, that French Catholics expect of Protestant Englishmen. A penniless wanderer, he had met Annette through chance encounter. Marriage to such a man was out of the question for a girl from a respectable family; better far that the child, when it arrived, should quietly be put out to nurse. This plan was adhered to. By the early autumn of 1792 Annette's relatives had made it impossible for the young couple to see one another. The lovers contrived a farewell meeting, during which Wordsworth kissed the clothes in the *layette* of his future child. Then he left for Paris, and England. The child, when born, was a girl; she was given the name Caroline and was brought up exclusively in France.

Wordsworth's guardians, when they learned of his indiscretion, were equally opposed to any idea of marriage. Only Dorothy was enthusiastic for William to wed Annette; she sent letters to Annette encouraging her to look forward to life in England, sharing a cottage with Caroline, William, and Dorothy too. All this dreaming and planning was brought to an end by the outbreak of war between France and

THIS PORTRAIT captures much of William Hazlitt's famous pen-portrait of the poet: "Gaunt and Don-Quixote-like . . . a fire in his eyes . . . and a convulsive inclination to laughter about the mouth, a good deal at variance with the solemn stately expression of the rest of his face."

England. Annette was left to rebuild her life as the so-called widowed Mrs Williams (*La Veuve Williams*) and to play an active and daring role as a counter-revolutionary in her own country.

A SISTER'S COMFORT

During the months following this unhappy affair, William passed through a period of profound dejection. Dorothy alone was able to comfort and cheer him. In the spring of 1794 brother and sister set out to visit the Lakes. They spent much of 1794 at Keswick staying at Windy Brow, the home of William's friend, Raisley Calvert, a youth who was dying of consumption. In the Lakes William became increasingly convinced that his true vocation in life was that of a poet. He could not dissipate his time and energies upon trying to earn a living. Nevertheless he could not live on air. If he and Dorothy were to spend the rest of their lives together, as they now planned to do, in some rustic retreat, an income would have to be obtained somehow.

Dorothy persuaded Raisley Calvert that William's poetic genius, if given full encouragement, would

one day "benefit mankind". But in order that he might give himself fully to poetry it was essential that he should be released from the pressures of everyday life. In October 1794 Calvert signed a will bequeathing William nine hundred pounds (worth, of course, a great deal more in those days than it is now). Invested, this would ensure a basic financial independence for William and Dorothy, his "Emma", or "Emmaline", as he always called her in his poetry.

> Long is it since we met to part no more,
> Since I and Emma heard each other's call
> And were companions once again . . .
> Two of a scattered brood that could not bear
> To live in loneliness; 'tis long since we,
> Remembering much and hoping more, found means
> To walk abreast, though in a narrow path,
> With undivided steps.
>
> *"Home at Grasmere"*

When Calvert died the following January and William came into his inheritance, brother and sister took up residence together first at Racedown, in Dorset, and then at Alfoxden, close to Nether Stowey, Somerset, where William's exciting new friend, Samuel Taylor Coleridge, was living with his wife and infant son, Hartley. As we have already learned, here the famous poetic partnership came into flower and a triumvirate of a particularly close and sensitive kind was cemented between William, Coleridge and Dorothy.

THE AGE OF IDEALISM

Theirs was a generation which was seeking realization of the Romantic idyll of a "new Earth and new Heaven", where all men should live in freedom, peace and equality within a philosophical ambience of Rousseauist Pantheism that saw the human mind

COLERIDGE, THE ROMANTIC IDEALIST, was determined that his infant son, Hartley, (b. 1796), should grow up to be at one with Nature in the best Rousseauist tradition – appreciating the wonders of the natural world and celebrating its regenerative effect on the mind of Man.

". . . For I was reared
In the great city, pent 'mid cloisters dim,
And saw nought lovely but the sky and stars.
But thou, my babe! shalt wander like a breeze
By lakes and sandy shores, beneath the crags
Of ancient mountain, and beneath the clouds . . ."
Samuel Taylor Coleridge: "Frost at Midnight"

as part of Nature and Nature as One with God; the ideal which originally inspired the French Revolution. This was why the Revolution (at least in its early stages) roused the strong sympathies of poets, writers and artists throughout Europe, North America and Britain – among them the three young men who, subsequently, were to become known as "the Lake Poets": Wordsworth, Coleridge and Robert Southey.

Recalling, in late middle age, what the French Revolution had meant to his generation, Southey wrote that few persons but those who had been young at the time could comprehend how the Revolution had opened a visionary world: "Old things seemed passing away, and nothing was dreamt of but the regeneration of the human race. Revolutionary France, for the radical British young, held all their wishes and expectations." To quote Wordworth:

> Bliss was it in that dawn to be alive,
> But to be young was very heaven...
> *"French Revolution as it Appeared to*
> *Enthusiasts at its Commencement"*

Southey and Coleridge had first met in June 1794, initially drawn together by poetry. Each shared a further interest; a vision of creating Utopia on earth. Southey dreamed of an island community where man might enjoy "the advantages and yet avoid the vices of cultivated society." Coleridge was equally enthusiastic for a society where individual property was abolished and liberty, equality and fraternity were observed under a participatory government by all and for all (which he called "Pantisocracy"). Within a month of getting to know each other the enthusiastic pair had thrashed out the leading features of a Pantisocracy, to be founded in America (which had recently become independent of the British Crown); the place of settlement to be Kentucky. A party of ladies and gentlemen, twelve of each sex, would depart for America the following April. They would support their community by their own labour and the produce of their industry would be property common to them all. They would assemble a good library, their leisure hours were to be spent in study, liberal discussion and the education of their children.

WINDY BROW, where Wordsworth tended the dying Raisley Calvert, his benefactor, later figured largely in the social life of the Coleridge and Wordsworth families at Greta Hall. The artist, the Reverend Joseph Wilkinson, a neighbour at Ormathwaite, was a prolific amateur painter.

It was calculated that if each gentleman provided £125 this would be a sufficient amount to carry the scheme into execution.

Two young women were rapidly lined up as partners for Southey and Coleridge respectively. These were sisters, Edith and Sara Fricker. Southey had recently got himself engaged to Edith; he was not in love with her (in fact he was on the rebound from a frustrated passion for another girl) but he saw in Edith the promise of a "meek and devoted partner" with whom his bruised heart might find "calm contentment". Sara, pretty, lively, accomplished, would make Coleridge an excellent partner, decided Southey. Coleridge, like Southey, maintained that a wife must possess humility. Mary Wollstonecraft's book, *A Vindication of the Rights of Woman*, had recently been published and radicals everywhere enthused over it, but while emancipated females battling for their rights were splendid in theory, they might not be relied upon to promote "domestic peace". Coleridge had never set eyes on Sara Fricker in his life, but doubtless assumed that if one sister was "the mild and retired kind" (as Southey assured him was the case with Edith) then the other sister would naturally be so too. Within weeks he had met Sara, she had fallen dizzily in love with him, he had proposed and had been accepted. Other ladies and gentleman were recruited for the "Pantisocratic Scheme" (as it was generally called). "Everything smiles upon our undertaking," announced Southey with satisfaction.

The intending emigrants had only the wildest notions of what America was like; romantic tales of Indians, savannahs and buffaloes mingled in their imagination with scenes of rural life such as they knew in Devon and Somerset. Southey dreamed of how: "When Coleridge and I are sawing down a tree we shall discuss metaphysics; criticise poetry when hunting a buffalo, and write sonnets whilst following the plough." Their final decision was for the banks of the Susquehannah, rather than Kentucky, and March was now fixed as their month of departure for the New World, in a "storm-tossed bark".

Although in this 1795 portrait, by Peter Vandyke, the 23-year-old Coleridge looks respectable enough, we know that at this point in his career he normally cultivated the appearance of a wild and unkempt revolutionary: his future bride described him, as cutting "a dreadful figure"; his clothes worn out and full of holes, his hair long and shaggy.

THE DREAM PERSISTS

But the scheme came to nothing. One by one of the intending Pantisocrats discovered excuses for opting out and finally Southey and Coleridge quarrelled. However Sara and Coleridge (he now as raptly in love with her as she was with him) were married in October 1795, while Southey and Edith married a month later. After living for a while in Bristol (Sara's birthplace and home town), where Coleridge wrote and published a radical newsheet, *The Watchman*, Sara and her Samuel, with their infant son, Hartley, moved to the little village of Nether Stowey, to be neighbours of their good and valued friend Thomas Poole. They planned to live an idealistic life in a leaky, dilapidated cottage they had discovered. Coleridge would abandon politics with which he was now thoroughly disillusioned, and instead would support his family with his spade (an implement which he had previously never handled in his entire life). In short, they would conduct a kind of mini-pantisocratic experiment of their own. Meantime Southey and Edith had gone to Portugal and, on their return, Southey commenced reading law. The brothers-in-law patched up their quarrel, at their wives' insistence.

The Coleridges made their move to Nether Stowey on the last day of the year 1796. Coleridge and Wordsworth had first met in September 1795 and had corresponded intermittently since that meeting, and in March 1797 Wordsworth and his friend Basil Montagu, on their way to Bristol from Racedown, visited the Coleridges in Stowey. Wordsworth was staying there again a month later, on his way back to Racedown, and in June, Coleridge went to Racedown to stay with William and Dorothy. Coleridge had soon persuaded brother and sister that they, too, should come to live near Nether Stowey and within weeks they had arrived to house-hunt in that neighbourhood. They declared that the Coleridgean abode (described by Coleridge in his franker moments as an "old hovel") was exactly what they themselves were looking for. In fact, when they did discover somewhere to live, at nearby Alfoxden, it was a large mansion in a deer park, "with furniture enough for a dozen families like ours," reported Dorothy.

The Coleridges and Wordsworths were not the only intellectual radicals attempting, at that period in time, to escape from the harsh realities of the outside world by retreating into the country. The collapse of

ALFOXDEN, three miles from Nether Stowey, lies between the Quantock Hills and the Bristol Channel. Dorothy Wordsworth's "Alfoxden Journal" describes her delight in the local scenery. A typical entry reads, "Went to the hill-top. Sat a considerable time overlooking the country towards the sea . . . The Welsh hills capped by a huge range of tumultuous white clouds. The sea, spotted with white, of a bluish grey in general, streaked with darker lines. The near shores clear; scattered farmhouses half-concealed by mossy orchards".

the French revolutionary dream of building a perfect new world; the terrible disillusionment of visionaries brought about by the September Massacres and the Terror in a France that had promised social equality, justice, and peace to all men; and the emergence of Napoleon and his imperial ambitions backed by a ruthless military strength banished completely the poetic Rousseauist dreams of Arcady. Or, *almost* banished them; those Romantics who could find a way to do so turned their backs upon what was going on and sought refuge in rusticity – an Arcadian landscape of their own.

Wordsworth, of course, had never been involved in the Pantisocratic venture; he had not known Coleridge at that time, and even had the two men then known each other it would have been unlikely that Wordsworth, a born solitary by nature, would have favoured a communal experiment of that sort. In France, where he had witnessed something of the Revolution at first hand, he had held himself aloof from the kind of active political involvement in which numerous other British subjects, aflame with republican and democratic sentiments, had engaged. There is evidence that he knew several revolutionary Frenchmen, and attended Jacobin gatherings in Blois, but he was (as his future sister-in-law, Sarah Hutchinson, was to remark) essentially a cautious personality and would seem to have held back from direct revolutionary action such as the more flamboyant of his compatriots embarked upon.

A POETIC AWAKENING

By the time Wordsworth had moved to Nether Stowey poetry, not politics, had become his paramount concern. At this stage of his career he was scarcely known as a poet, save to a discerning few, whereas Coleridge was generally recognized as one of the foremost poets of his generation: two years younger than Wordsworth in actual years, he was, as it were, senior in achievement, erudition, literary experience and reputation. He had published, in 1794 (in collaboration with Southey), a poetic drama, *The Fall of Robespierre*, and 1796 had seen the appearance of his *Poems on Various Subjects* and *Ode to the Departing Year*. Yet, despite all this apparent success, Coleridge was still struggling to find his true, great voice as a poet and learnt much from his study of Wordsworth's *An Evening Walk* and its accompanying poem, *Descriptive Sketches*. Coleridge particularly admired Wordsworth's "form, style and manner" and "novelty of . . . images, acting in conjunction with style." Resultantly, in his latest work, Coleridge was attempting composition where texture was as important a technique to consider as was metre.

Wordsworth for his part greatly admired Coleridge's poetry, as well as his force of creative genius (apparent, indeed, to all who met him) and marvellous gifts of conversation, range of mind and capacity for original, deeply penetrative thought. All this had a profound and immediate effect upon Wordsworth. Moreover, in addition, Coleridge's wit and high spirits, his sheer gusto for life made him

THIS MINIATURE PORTRAIT by an unknown artist is believed to be a keepsake portrait of Dorothy Wordsworth as a young woman, given by her niece Dora to Maria Jane Jewsbury; a youthful poetess who, in 1825, presented Wordsworth with a copy of her verses, dedicated to him. During a stay at Rydal Mount she formed a great admiration for Dorothy Wordsworth and developed lasting friendships with Dora Wordsworth and Sara Coleridge fille. Apart from a silhouette portrait now in the possession of Dove Cottage, this is the only surviving portrait of Dorothy in her youth. It certainly agrees with her self-description as having a "wishy-washy" complexion and wearing her hair curled about her face "in light curls frizzed at the bottom and turned at the end." Here, too, are the dark eyes with their "shooting lights" immortalized in "Lines Written . . . Above Tintern Abbey."

enormous fun to be with: to quote Wordsworth's description of him, "Noisy he was, and gamesome as a boy." Coleridge's exuberance acted upon Wordsworth like a series of beneficial electric shocks. In no time at all the two men, each so different in temperament, were mutually stimulated to make prodigious strides in their poetry; a bursting forth of hitherto burgeoning genius into full flower, almost overnight.

Together the two poets took long walks, deep in conversation as they wandered. Dorothy, who accompanied them, was able to make her own important contributions, for she was gifted with an "eye watchful in minutest observation of nature" (to quote Coleridge) and a wonderful facility with words, always able to say precisely what she wanted to say, in the simplest and yet the most effective manner. She was already keeping a journal describing what she saw on her country rambles; accounts of the country people she met. These journals she wrote not for publication, but to give her brother pleasure, and to remind him of scenes they had enjoyed together, and incidents that they had shared as they viewed and appreciated nature. Many of the things which she observed and noted in her journal (which Coleridge as well as Wordsworth, was allowed to see) provided the poets with important images: a famous instance is the lone leaf left on a tree: "The sole remaining leaf – danced round and round like a rag blown by the wind," she noted; an image which Coleridge later used in *Christabel*,

> The one red leaf, the last of its clan,
> That dances as often as dance it can,
> Hanging so light, and hanging so high,
> On the topmost twig that looks up at the sky.

One one occasion, while writing a description of a wintry scene, in his own notebooks, he breaks off, unable to put something the way he wants to: "Ask Dorothy for a word," he jots.

During that marvellous year between the mid-summers of 1797 and 1798 Coleridge wrote his greatest poetry: his miraculous *Kubla Khan*; his masterpiece, *The Ancient Mariner*; Part One of *Christabel*; and his unique conversation poems, blending poetry with philosophical rumination: *This Lime Tree Bower, Frost at Midnight, Fears in Solitude, The Nightingale*. Wordsworth likewise produced a torrent of poems. The Wordsworth who had written *An Evening Walk* had been a somewhat dandyish and fashion-conscious youth, impartially dividing his attention between his tutor and his tailor. The Hawkshead schoolboy, solitary roamer of the hills and vales, already a poet in spirit, as an under-graduate "slipped into the ordinary works of careless youth", enjoying,

> . . . Companionships,
> Friendships, acquaintances . . .
> We sauntered, played, or rioted; we talked
> Unprofitable talk at morning hours;
> Drifted about along the streets and walks,
> Read lazily in trivial books . . .
> *"The Prelude" 1805 Book III*

as Wordsworth later described his life at Cambridge. When he had occasionally turned to Nature and to poetry, it had been as a fashionably dedicated devotee of the Picturesque School, a true disciple of Gilpin.

Gradually he had matured in his attitude and now, under the influence of Coleridge, Wordsworth changed even more, learning,

> To look on nature, not as in the hour
> Of thoughtless youth, but hearing oftentimes
> The still, sad music of humanity.
> *"Lines Written . . . Above Tintern Abbey"*

Early in November 1797, Coleridge, Dorothy and William made a coast-line walking tour along the fringes of Exmoor, between Watchet and Linton. During this walk, in the strange way that inspiration works, the Ancient Mariner arrived, to being his imperishable tale, " 'There was a ship!' " Soon the storm-blast was chasing the vessel to the South Pole,

> And ice, mast--high, came floating by,
> As green as emerald . . .

and out of the polar fog, on vast pinions, the Albatross came flying.

THE COLLABORATION OF GENIUS

At first *The Ancient Mariner* was to be published as a separate poem, it being exclusively the work of Coleridge, owing only to Wordsworth the suggestion that the Ancient Mariner should shoot the albatross. However, following the completion of this poem, Coleridge and Wordsworth began working to a dual plan of composition. Wordsworth selected subjects from ordinary life, to which he proposed to give "the charm of novelty . . . by [directing] the mind's attention . . . to the loveliness and the wonders of the world before us," while Coleridge concentrated upon "persons and characters supernatural, or at least romantic", to be used in poems intended to procure "for these shadows of imagination that willing suspension of disbelief, for the moment, which constitutes poetic faith."

The poems resulting from this collaboration were published, including *The Ancient Mariner*, in 1798, as *Lyrical Ballads*, one of the most famous and influential volumes of poetry ever to appear in the English language – though, at the time, these poems were so much in advance of public taste that,

"And through the drifts the snowy clifts
Did send a dismal sheen:
Nor shapes of men nor beats we ken –
The ice was all between . . .

At length did cross an Albatross,
Through the fog it came . . ."

Samuel Taylor Coleridge:
"The Rime of the Ancient Mariner"

---

generally speaking, they had nothing but derision heaped upon them. *The Ancient Mariner* (destined to become one of the most famous poems ever written) had, in particular, scorn and abuse poured upon it. The most admired poem in the collection was Wordsworth's *Lines Written . . . Above Tintern Abbey*; a last minute inclusion, composed between July 10th and 13th, 1798, when the rest of *Lyrical*

Ballads was already at the press. *Frost at Midnight*, considered as unsuitable for the book, was published separately; *Kubla Khan* was not published until many years later.

POETS IN EXILE

By the time *Lyrical Ballads* appeared, Coleridge and the Wordsworths were in Germany. Wordsworth, at Alfoxden, had made no secret of his republican sympathies, while Coleridge, of course, was an established and well known radical speaker and journalist. The natives of Stowey decided that here were French spies: as a result of the ensuing local talk and excitement the two poets were investigated by government security officers, sent down to Stowey for that purpose. No arrest resulted, but the owner of Alfoxden House refused to extend Wordsworth's tenancy.

KUBLA KHAN

In Xanadu did Kubla Khan
A stately pleasure-dome decree:
Where Alph, the sacred river, ran
Through caverns measureless to man
  Down to a sunless sea.
So twice five miles of fertile ground
With walls and towers were girdled round:
And there were gardens bright with sinuous rills
Where blossomed many an incense-bearing tree;
And here were forests ancient as the hills,
Enfolding sunny spots of greenery.

But oh! that deep romantic chasm which slanted
Down the green hill athwart a cedarn cover!
A savage place! as holy and enchanted
As e'er beneath a waning moon was haunted
By woman wailing for her demon-lover!
And from this chasm, with ceaseless turmoil seething,
As if this earth in fast thick pants were breathing,
A mighty fountain momently was forced:
Amid whose swift half-intermitted burst
Huge fragments vaulted like rebounding hail,
Or chaffy grain beneath the thresher's flail:
And mid these dancing rocks at once and ever
It flung up momently the sacred river.
Five miles meandering with a mazy motion
Through wood and dale the sacred river ran,

Then reached the caverns measureless to man,
And sank in tumult to a lifeless ocean:
And 'mid this tumult Kubla heard from far
Ancestral voices prophesying war!

  The shadow of the dome of pleasure
  Floated midway on the waves;
  Where was heard the mingled measure
  From the fountain and the caves.
It was a miracle of rare device,
A sunny pleasure-dome with caves of ice!

  A damsel with a dulcimer
  In a vision once I saw:
  It was an Abyssinian maid,
  And on her dulcimer she played,
  Singing of Mount Abora.
  Could I revive within me
  Her symphony and song,
  To such a deep delight 'twould win me
That with music loud and long,
I would build that dome in air,
That sunny dome! those caves of ice!
And all who heard should see them there,
And all should cry, Beware! Beware!
His flashing eyes, his floating hair!
Weave a circle round him thrice,
And close your eyes with holy dread,
For he on honey-dew hath fed,
And drunk the milk of Paradise.

Samuel Taylor Coleridge

LINES WRITTEN . . . ABOVE TINTERN ABBEY

Five years have passed; five summers, with the length
Of five long winters! and again I hear
These waters, rolling from their mountain-springs
With a sweet inland murmur. Once again
Do I behold these steep and lofty cliffs,
Which on a wild secluded scene impress
Thoughts of more deep seclusion; and connect
The landscape with the quiet of the sky.
The day is come when I again repose
Here, under this dark sycamore, and view
These plots of cottage-ground, these orchard-tufts,
Which, at this season, with their unripe fruits,
Are clad in one green hue, and lose themselves
Among the woods and copses, nor disturb
The wild green landscape. Once again I see
These hedge-rows—hardly hedge-rows, little lines
Of sportive wood run wild; these pastoral farms
Green to the very door; and wreaths of smoke
Sent up, in silence, from among the trees,
With some uncertain notice, as might seem,
Of vagrant dwellers in the houseless woods,
Or of some hermit's cave, where by his fire
The hermit sits alone.

        Though absent long,
These forms of beauty have not been to me
As is a landscape to a blind man's eye;
But oft, in lonely rooms, and 'mid the din
Of towns and cities, I have owed to them,
In hours of weariness, sensations sweet,
Felt in the blood, and felt along the heart,
And passing even into my purer mind
With tranquil restoration:—feelings too
Of unremembered pleasure: such, perhaps,
As may have had no trivial influence
On that best portion of a good man's life,
His little, nameless, unremembered acts
Of kindness and of love. Nor less, I trust,
To them I may have owed another gift,
Of aspect more sublime: that blessed mood
In which the burthen of the mystery,
In which the heavy and the weary weight
Of all this unintelligible world
Is lightened; that serene and blessed mood
In which the affections gently lead us on
Until, the breath of this corporeal frame
And even the motion of our human blood
Almost suspended, we are laid asleep
In body, and become a living soul;
While with an eye made quiet by the power
Of harmony, and the deep power of joy,
We see into the life of things.

              If this
Be but a vain belief, yet, oh! how oft,
In darkness, and amid the many shapes
Of joyless daylight; when the fretful stir
Unprofitable, and the fever of the world,
Have hung upon the beatings of my heart,
How oft, in spirit, have I turned to thee,
O sylvan Wye! Thou wanderer through the woods,
How often has my spirit turned to thee!

And now, with gleams of half-extinguished thought,
With many recognitions dim and faint,
And somewhat of a sad perplexity,
The picture of the mind revives again:
While here I stand, not only with the sense
Of present pleasure, but with pleasing thoughts
That in this moment there is life and food
For future years. And so I dare to hope,
Though changed, no doubt, from what I was when first
I came among these hills: when like a roe
I bounded o'er the mountains, by the sides
Of the deep rivers, and the lonely streams,
Wherever nature led; more like a man
Flying from something that he dreads, than one
Who sought the thing he loved. For nature then
(The coarser pleasures of my boyish days
And their glad animal movements all gone by)
To me was all in all.—I cannot paint
What then I was. The sounding cataract
Haunted me like a passion; the tall rock,
The mountain, and the deep and gloomy wood,
Their colours and their forms, were then to me
An appetite: a feeling and a love,
That had no need of a remoter charm
By thought supplied, or any interest
Unborrowed from the eye.—That time is past,
And all its aching joys are now no more,
And all its dizzy raptures. Not for this
Faint I, nor mourn nor murmur; other gifts
Have followed, for such loss, I would believe,
Abundant recompense. For I have learned
To look on nature, not as in the hour
Of thoughtless youth, but hearing oftentimes
The still, sad music of humanity,
Nor harsh nor grating, though of ample power
To chasten and subdue. And I have felt
A presence that disturbs me with the joy
Of elevated thoughts: a sense sublime
Of something far more deeply interfused,
Whose dwelling is the light of setting suns,
And the round ocean and the living air,
And the blue sky, and in the mind of man;
A motion and a spirit, that impels
All thinking things, all objects of all thought,
And rolls through all things.—Therefore am I still
A lover of the meadows and the woods
And mountains; and of all that we behold
From this green earth; of all the mighty world
Of eye and ear, both what they half create
And what perceive; well pleased to recognise
In nature and the language of the sense

The anchor of my purest thoughts, the nurse,
The guide, the guardian of my heart, and soul
Of all my moral being.

              Nor, perchance,
If I were not thus taught, should I the more
Suffer my genial spirits to decay:
For thou art with me, here, upon the banks
Of this fair river; thou, my dearest friend,
My dear, dear friend, and in thy voice I catch
The language of my former heart, and read
My former pleasures in the shooting lights
Of thy wild eyes. Oh! yet a little while
May I behold in thee what I was once,
My dear, dear sister! And this prayer I make,
Knowing that Nature never did betray
The heart that loved her; 'tis her privilege,
Through all the years of this our life, to lead
From joy to joy: for she can so inform
The mind that is within us, so impress
With quietness and beauty, and so feed
With lofty thoughts, that neither evil tongues,
Rash judgments, nor the sneers of selfish men,
Nor greetings where no kindness is, nor all
The dreary intercourse of daily life,
Shall e'er prevail against us, or disturb
Our cheerful faith that all which we behold

Is full of blessings. Therefore let the moon
Shine on thee in thy solitary walk;
And let the misty mountain winds be free
To blow against thee: and, in after years,
When these wild ecstasies shall be matured
Into a sober pleasure, when thy mind
Shall be a mansion for all lovely forms,
Thy memory be as a dwelling-place
For all sweet sounds and harmonies; oh! then,
If solitude, or fear, or pain, or grief
Should be thy portion, with what healing thoughts
Of tender joy wilt thou remember me,
And these my exhortations! Nor, perchance,
If I should be where I no more can hear
Thy voice, nor catch from thy wild eyes these gleams
Of past existence, wilt thou then forget
That on the banks of this delightful stream
We stood together; and that I, so long
A worshipper of Nature, hither came
Unwearied in that service: rather say
With warmer love, oh! with far deeper zeal
Of holier love. Nor wilt thou then forget
That after many wanderings, many years
Of absence, these steep woods and lofty cliffs,
And this green pastoral landscape, were to me
More dear, both for themselves and for thy sake.

William Wordsworth

FROST AT MIDNIGHT

The frost performs its secret ministry,
Unhelped by any wind. The owlet's cry
Came loud—and hark, again! loud as before.
The inmates of my cottage, all at rest,
Have left me to that solitude, which suits
Abstruser musings: save that at my side
My cradled infant slumbers peacefully.
'Tis calm indeed! so calm, that it disturbs
And vexes meditation with its strange
And extreme silentness. Sea, hill, and wood,
This populous village! Sea, and hill, and wood,
With all the numberless goings on of life,
Inaudible as dreams! the thin blue flame
Lies on my low burnt fire, and quivers not;
Only that film, which fluttered on the grate,
Still flutters there, the sole unquiet thing.
Methinks, its motion in this hush of nature
Gives it dim sympathies with me who live,

Making it a companionable form,
Whose puny flaps and freaks the idling Spirit
By its own moods interprets, every where
Echo or mirror seeking of itself,
And makes a toy of Thought.

But O! how oft,
How oft, at school, with most believing mind,
Presageful, have I gazed upon the bars,
To watch that fluttering stranger! and as oft
With unclosed lids, already had I dreamt
Of my sweet birth-place, and the old church-tower,
Whose bells, the poor man's only music, rang
From morn to evening, all the hot Fair-day,
So sweetly, that they stirred and haunted me
With a wild pleasure, falling on mine ear
Most like articulate sounds of things to come!
So gazed I, till the soothing things I dreamt
Lulled me to sleep, and sleep prolonged my dreams!
And so I brooded all the following morn,
Awed by the stern preceptor's face, mine eye

Fixed with mock study on my swimming book:
Save if the door half opened, and I snatched
A hasty glance, and still my heart leaped up,
For still I hoped to see the stranger's face,
Townsman, or aunt, or sister more beloved,
My play-mate when we both were clothed alike!

Dear Babe, that sleepest cradled by my side,
Whose gentle breathings, heard in this deep calm,
Fill up the interspersed vacancies
And momentary pauses of the thought!
My babe so beautiful! it thrills my heart
With tender gladness, thus to look at thee,
And think that thou shalt learn far other lore
And in far other scenes! For I was reared
In the great city, pent 'mid cloisters dim,
And saw nought lovely but the sky and stars.
But thou, my babe! shalt wander like a breeze
By lakes and sandy shores, beneath the crags
Of ancient mountain, and beneath the clouds,
Which image in their bulk both lakes and shores

And mountain crags: so shalt thou see and hear
The lovely shapes and sounds intelligible
Of that eternal language, which thy God
Utters, who from eternity doth teach
Himself in all, and all things in himself.
Great universal Teacher! he shall mould
Thy spirit, and by giving make it ask.

Therefore all seasons shall be sweet to thee,
Whether the summer clothe the general earth
With greenness, or the redbreast sit and sing
Betwixt the tufts of snow on the bare branch
Of mossy apple-tree, while the nigh thatch
Smokes in the sun-thaw; whether the eve-drops fall
Heard only in the trances of the blast,
Or if the secret ministry of frost
Shall hang them up in silent icicles,
Quietly shining to the quiet Moon.

Samuel Taylor Coleridge

Coleridge having now been given a comfortable annuity by the Wedgwoods (notable patrons of science and the arts) decided to go to Germany for a few months; the Wordsworths accompanying him to Hamburg, and then leaving him. Alone together in their lodgings at Goslar, cut off from the outside world by the snow and ice of the worst winter of the century, brother and sister relished their solitude and William experienced another great upsurge of poetic power. He composed the mysteriously beautiful and evocative "Lucy" poems, inspired by his Muse, Dorothy: "Lucy" being Dorothy set in imagination in a dream-like Lakes setting; a wild child of Nature; an image, rather than a real girl. Together with the "Lucy" poems came the wonderful boyhood passages of *The Prelude*, opening with stanzas invoking his earliest years at Cockermouth, his birthplace.

A HOME AT GRASMERE

The first snow-and-storm besieged weeks at Grasmere were, for brother and sister, strongly reminiscent of their winter in Goslar; alone among strangers, shut away from the outside world, William compared himself and Dorothy to a pair of swans that were wintering on the lake,

> A lonely pair of milk-white Swans . . .
>   . . . From afar
> They came, like Emma and myself, to live
> Together here in peace and solitude,
> Choosing this Valley, they who had the choice
> Of the whole world.

Dorothy and he loved the swans,

> Not only for their beauty and their still
> And placid way of life and faithful love
> Inseparable, not for these alone,
> But that their state so much resembled ours;
> They also having chosen this abode;
> They strangers, and we strangers; they a pair,
> And we a solitary pair like them.
>
> *"Home at Grasmere"*

DURING THEIR FIRST COLD WINTER in Dove cottage, William and Dorothy lived in contented isolation, like the pair of swans they had seen wintering on the lake at Grasmere.

'STRANGE FITS OF PASSION
I HAVE KNOWN'

Strange fits of passion I have known:
And I will dare to tell,
But in the lover's ear alone,
What once to me befell.

When she I loved was strong and gay
And like a rose in June,
I to her cottage bent my way,
Beneath the evening moon.

Upon the moon I fixed my eye,
All over the wide lea;
My horse trudged on — and we drew nigh
Those paths so dear to me.

And now we reached the orchard plot;
And, as we climbed the hill,
Towards the roof of Lucy's cot
The moon descended still.

In one of those sweet dreams I slept,
Kind Nature's gentlest boon!
And, all the while, my eyes I kept
On the descending moon.

My horse moved on; hoof after hoof
He raised, and never stopped:
When down behind the cottage roof
At once the planet dropped.

What fond and wayward thoughts will slide
Into a lover's head —
'O Mercy!' to myself I cried,
'If Lucy should be dead!'

William Wordsworth

'SHE DWELT AMONG
TH' UNTRODDEN WAYS'

She dwelt among th' untrodden ways
    Beside the springs of Dove,
A maid whom there were none to praise,
    And very few to love.

A violet by a mossy stone
    Half-hidden from the eye!
– Fair as a star, when only one
    Is shining in the sky.

She lived unknown, and few could know
    When Lucy ceased to be;
But she is in her grave, and oh!
    The difference to me.

William Wordsworth

'A SLUMBER DID MY SPIRIT SEAL'

A slumber did my spirit seal;
    I had no human fears:
She seemed a thing that could not feel
    The touch of earthly years.

No motion has she now, no force;
    She neither hears nor sees,
Rolled round in earth's diurnal course
    With rocks and stones and trees.

William Wordsworth

INFANCY AND CHILDHOOD

(excerpts from "The Prelude" 1798–1799)

_____

Was it for this
That one, the fairest of all rivers, loved
To blend his murmurs with my Nurse's song,
And from his alder shades, and rocky falls,
And from his fords and shallows, sent a voice
That flowed along my dreams? For this didst thou
O Derwent, travelling over the green plains
Near my "sweet birth-place," didst thou beauteous Stream
Make ceaseless music through the night and day,
Which with its steady cadence tempering
Our human waywardness, composed my thoughts
To more than infant softness, giving me,
Among the fretful dwellings of mankind,
A knowledge, a dim earnest of the calm
Which Nature breathes among the fields and groves?
　　Beloved Derwent! fairest of all Streams!
Was it for this that I, a four year's child,
A naked Boy, among thy silent pools
Made one long bathing of a summer's day?
Basked in the sun, or plunged into thy streams,
Alternate, all a summer's day, or coursed
Over the sandy fields, and dashed the flowers
Of yellow grunsel, or when crag and hill,
The woods and distant Skiddaw's lofty height
Were bronzed with a deep radiance, stood alone,
A naked Savage in the thunder showers? . . .
　　The mind of man is fashioned and built up
Even as a strain of music: I believe
That there are spirits, which, when they would form
A favored being, from his very dawn
Of infancy do open out the clouds
As at the touch of lightning, seeking him
With gentle visitation: quiet Powers!
Retired and seldom recognized, yet kind,
And to the very meanest not unknown;
With me, though rarely, in my early days
They communed: others too there are who use,
Yet haply aiming at the self-same end,
Severer interventions, ministry
More palpable, and of their school was I.
　　They guided me: one evening, led by them,
I went alone into a Shepherd's boat,
A skiff that to a willow-tree was tied
Within a rocky cave, its usual home;
The moon was up, the lake was shining clear
Among the hoary mountains: from the shore
I pushed, and struck the oars, and struck again
In cadence, and my little Boat moved on
Just like a man who walks with stately step
Though bent on speed. It was an act of stealth
And troubled pleasure; not without the voice
Of mountain-echoes did my boat move on,
Leaving behind her still on either side

Small circles glittering idly in the moon
Until they melted all into one track
Of sparkling light. A rocky steep uprose
Above the cavern of the willow tree,
And now, as suited one who proudly rowed
With his best skill, I fixed a steady view
Upon the top of that same craggy ridge,
The bound of the horizon, for behind
Was nothing — but the stars and the grey sky.
— She was an elfin pinnace; twenty times
I dipped my oars into the silent lake,

And, as I rose upon the stroke, my Boat
Went heaving through the water, like a swan —
When from behind that rocky steep, till then
The bound of the horizon, a huge Cliff,
As if with voluntary power instinct,
Upreared its head: I struck, and struck again,
And, growing still in stature, the huge cliff
Rose up between me and the stars, and still
With measured motion, like a living thing,
Strode after me. With trembling hands I turned,
And through the silent water stole my way

Back to the cavern of the willow-tree.
There, in her mooring-place I left my bark,
And through the meadows homeward went with grave
And serious throughts: and after I had seen
That spectacle, for many days my brain
Worked with a dim and undetermined sense
Of unknown modes of being: in my thoughts
There was a darkness, call it solitude
Or blank desertion; no familiar shapes
Of hourly objects, images of trees,
Of sea or sky, no colours of green fields:

But huge and mighty forms, that do not live
Like living men, moved slowly through my mind
By day, and were the trouble of my dreams.
    Ah! not in vain ye Beings of the hills!
And ye that walk the woods and open heaths
By moon or star-light, thus from my first dawn
Of childhood did ye love to intertwine
The passions that build up our human soul,
Not with the mean and vulgar works of man,
But with high objects, with eternal things,

With life and nature, purifying thus
The elements of feeling and of thought,
And sanctifying by such discipline
Both pain and fear, until we recognise
A grandeur in the beatings of the heart.
    Nor was this fellowship vouchsafed to me
With stinted kindness. In November days,
When vapours, rolling down the valleys, made
A lonely scene more lonesome, among woods
At noon, and 'mid the calm of summer nights

When by the margin of the trembling lake
Beneath the gloomy hills I homeward went
In solitude, such intercourse was mine.
    And in the frosty season when the sun
Was set, and, visible for many a mile,
The cottage windows through the twilight blazed,
I heeded not the summons: clear and loud
The village clock tolled six; I wheeled about
Proud and exulting like an untired horse
That cares not for its home. — All shod with steel
We hissed along the polished ice, in games
Confederate, imitative of the chace
And woodland pleasures, the resounding horn,
The pack loud bellowing, and the hunted hare.
So through the darkness and the cold we flew,
And not a voice was idle: with the din,
Meanwhile, the precipices rang aloud,
The leafless trees and every icy crag
Tinkled like iron, while the distant hills
Into the tumult sent an alien sound
Of melancholy not unnoticed while the stars,
Eastward, were sparkling clear, and in the west
The orange sky of evening died away.
    Not seldom from the uproar I retired
Into a silent bay, or sportively
Glanced sideway leaving the tumultuous throng
To cut across the shadow of a star
That gleamed upon the ice: and oftentimes
When we had given our bodies to the wind
And all the shadowy banks on either side
Came sweeping through the darkness, spinning still

The rapid line of motion, then at once
Have I, reclining back upon my heels,
Stopped short; yet still the solitary cliffs
Wheeled by me, even as if the earth had rolled
With visible motion her diurnal round;
Behind me did they stretch in solemn train
Feebler and feebler, and I stood and watched
Till all was tranquil as a summer sea. . .
    Yes, I remember when the changeful earth
And twice five seasons on my mind had stamped
The faces of the moving year, even then,
A Child, I held unconscious intercourse
With the eternal Beauty, drinking in
A pure organic pleasure from the lines
Of curling mist or from the level plain
Of waters coloured by the steady clouds.
    The sands of Westmoreland, the creeks and bays
Of Cumbria's rocky limits, they can tell
How when the sea threw off his evening shade
And to the Shepherd's hut beneath the crags
Did send sweet notice of the rising moon,
How I have stood to images like these
A stranger, linking with the spectacle
No body of associated forms
And bringing with me no peculiar sense
Of quietness or peace, yet I have stood
Even while my eye has moved o'er three long leagues
Of shining water, gathering, as it seemed,
Through the wide surface of that field of light
New pleasure, like a bee among the flowers.

William Wordsworth

"For I would walk alone,
. . . listening to notes that are
The ghostly language of the ancient earth,
Or make their dim abode in distant winds."

William Wordsworth:
"The Prelude" 1805 Book II

While Dorothy slaved at making curtains and binding rugs and carpets, William, after his initial burst of painting and wall-papering, roamed the hills. The beauty of the snow-covered landscape, whether gleaming in morning sunshine "like a mountain built of silver light", or dramatically sombre under a sunset sky, filled him with daylong wonder and delight. When the weather was too wild for walking, he sheltered in a fir grove looking across Grasmere to Silver Howe. Even when daylight had waned he lingered out of doors, spellbound by the magical beauty of the place,

> . . . for I would walk alone,
> Under the quiet stars . . .
> . . . and I would stand,
> If the night blackened with a coming storm,

Beneath some rock, listening to notes that are
The ghostly language of the ancient earth,
Or make their dim abode in distant winds.

"The Prelude" 1850 Book II

Yet, lonely and mysterious as the mountains were, however pregnant the nights with druidical murmurs and the voices of rocks and stones and distant winds, daylight revealed a touching witness to the generations of men who had made this region their home from earliest times,

> Look where we will, some human heart has been
> Before us with its offering . . .

"Home at Grasmere"

The cottages and little homesteads seeming, as Wordsworth was fond of saying, "to have grown rather than to have been erected; – to have risen, by

". . . the bleak music from the old stone wall . . ."

William Wordsworth:
"The Prelude" 1805 Book XII

THESE TYPICAL LAKE COUNTRY COTTAGES, in a watercolour by W.J. Blacklock, are a wonderful example of Wordsworth's description, in his "Guide to the Lakes", of "little homesteads seeming to have grown rather than to have been erected; – to have risen, by an instinct of their own, out of the native rock."

an instinct of their own, out of the native rock"; with endless dry-stone walls intersecting the dale bottoms to fashion innumerable little fields and enclosures, or clambering over the fellsides to create protected grazing grounds, or running for miles over the tops, marking the boundaries of sheep-heafs and commons; little stone outhouses or shippens, places of shelter for the sheep in tempestuous weather; and

the little stone folds, found in the remotest and wildest of spots, again to provide shelter for the ewes and their lambs. The ancient pack-horse routes, contoured, causeyed and, over wetter ground, roughly metalled with local stone, with here and there along the way some simple shelter for the drovers; the valleys interlaced by innumerable little lanes and pathways leading from house to house and field to field; simple byways protected from driving winds and rain by more stone walls and lines of hawthorns grown bent and twisted by the blast. Little steeply arched bridges over the becks and torrents; "Monuments to the skill of our ancestors, and of that happy instinct by which consummate beauty was produced," as Wordsworth was to write in his famous *Guide to the Lakes*. Everywhere these simple objects of rustic architecture, all built to serve a purpose, yet each adding a harmony of its own to the overall beauty of the landscape, greeted the eye: buildings which, said Wordsworth, "in their very form call to mind the processes of Nature . . . [and] appear to be received into the bosom of the living principle of things . . . and affectingly direct the thoughts to that tranquil course of Nature and simplicity, along which the humble-minded inhabitants have, through so many generations, been led."

Then as now the shepherds and flockmasters of these valleys pursued patterns of working life dictated by the elements and the seasons and, fundamentally, differing very little, if at all, from the medieval experience of their forefathers. For Wordsworth the miraculously unspoiled Grasmere was, "A termination, and a last retreat." If he could not find Arcady here, then he could find it nowhere. Already, he was convinced that, here, he had found his Utopia. Grasmere as a true, unblemished centre, ". . . a Whole without dependence or defect . . . Unity entire." Reality here was more real than anywhere else; life quickened with a sap undiscoverable elsewhere,

> This whole Vale
> Home of untutored shepherds as it is,
> Swarms with sensation, as with gleams of sunshine,
> Shadows or breezes, scents or sounds.

Man here was Man; if not as he had been before his Fall, at least in a state of near-unimpaired and natural nobility,

> . . . As these lofty barriers break the force
> Of winds – this deep vale as it doth in part
> Conceal us from the storm – so here there is
> A Power and a protection for the mind . . .
> Substantial virtues have a firmer tone
> Than in the base and ordinary world.
>
> *"Home at Grasmere"*

And looking round this little Paradise, Wordsworth burst into a paean of rapture, almost approaching euphoria,

"This whole Vale . . .
Swarms with sensation, as with gleams of sunshine,
Shadows or breezes, scents or sounds."

William Wordsworth: "Home at Grasmere"

The boon is absolute; surpassing grace
To me hath been vouchsafed; among the bowers
Of blissful Eden this was neither given
Nor could be given, possession of the good
Which had been sighed for, ancient thought fulfilled,
And dear Imagination realised,
Up to their highest measure, yea and more.
"Home at Grasmere"

Of course he knew that the Lake Country shepherds were prone to human weakness, like any other mortals. He had spent his boyhood and early youth among them and he was perfectly aware that from time to time they drank and fought and swore, just as other men did. But this said, he recognized them as a remarkable breed of men, with more than a touch of the archetypal about them. It was possible to believe that here were shepherds who, while they watched their flocks at night, suddenly saw the angel of the Lord appear amongst them, while glory shone around. Even as a child Wordsworth had been fascinated by shepherds; had observed them, studied them, respected them; revered them, almost. His feelings for them persisted still and it is no wonder that much of his finest poetry was written about them.

A POETIC DUTY

The beauty of the country in which he now was living, the unaffected but impressive qualities of his humble neighbours, convinced him that it was incumbent upon him (and would be upon Coleridge too when he joined him in this Arcady) to measure up to this exalted environment. But something more than this: Wordsworth became increasingly convinced of his own poetic genius and of the obligation which this placed upon him to develop his great gift and use it for the benefit of other people.

Possessions have I, wholly, solely mine,
Something within, which yet is shared by none —
Not even the nearest to me and most dear —
Something which power and effort may impart.
I would impart it; I would spread it wide,
Immortal in the world which is to come.
"Home at Grasmere"

His shepherd neighbours, and himself the Poet, he perceived as linked together in the shared apprehension of a miracle. He wrote now of the shepherd, now of the Poet.

'IF THOU INDEED DERIVE THY LIGHT FROM HEAVEN'

If thou indeed derive thy light from Heaven,
Then, to the measure of that heaven-born light,
Shine, Poet! in thy place, and be content:—
The stars pre-eminent in magnitude,
And they that from the zenith dart their beams,
(Visible though they be to half the earth,
Though half a sphere be conscious of their brightness)
Are yet of no diviner origin,
No purer essence, than the one that burns,
Like an untended watch-fire, on the ridge
Of some dark mountain; or than those which seem
Humbly to hang, like twinkling winter lamps,
Among the branches of the leafless trees;
All are the undying offspring of one Sire:
Then, to the measure of the light vouchsafed,
Shine, Poet! in thy place, and be content.

William Wordsworth

SPRINGTIME IN GRASMERE

Winter gradually gave way to spring:

The birch tree woods
Are hung with thousand thousand diamond drops
Of melted hoar-frost . . .

"Home at Grasmere"

Everything shone and sparkled; water was running and singing everywhere, released by the melting ice. Birds sang, or wheeled and soared in the sky. "The gates of Spring are opened."

Brother John had now come to stay. Being a sailor he was wonderfully practical and handy; he did innumerable odd jobs about the cottage and helped to plant the garden. He was an enthusiastic walker and angler and, like his brother, enjoyed hours of solitude on the fells. On squally days, it was now his turn to take refuge in the fir grove. "John," Coleridge had said on meeting him, "is one of us", albeit he was "a *silent* poet"; inasmuch as he felt and thought and

ON THE MOUNTAIN TOPS

(excerpt from "The Ruined Cottage")

. . .Ere his ninth summer he was sent abroad
To tend his father's sheep, such was his task
Henceforward till the later day of youth.
Oh! then what soul was his when on the tops
Of the high mountains he beheld the sun
Rise up and bathe the world in light. He looked,
The ocean and the earth beneath him lay
In gladness and deep joy. The clouds were touched
And in their silent faces did he read

Unutterable love. Sound needed none
Nor any voice of joy; his spirit drank
The spectacle. Sensation, soul and form
All melted into him. They swallowed up
His animal being; in them did he live
And by them did he live. They were his life.
In such access of mind, in such high hour
Of visitation from the living God,
He did not feel the God; he felt his works;
Thought was not. In enjoyment it expired.
Such hour by prayer or praise was unprofaned,
He neither prayed, nor offered thanks or praise,
His mind was a thanksgiving to the power

That made him. It was blessedness and love.
A shepherd on the lonely mountain tops,
Such intercourse was his, and in this sort
Was his existence oftentimes possessed.
Ah! *then* how beautiful, how bright appeared
The written promise; he had early learned
To reverence the volume which displays
The mystery, the life which cannot die;
But in the mountains did he *feel* his faith
There did he see the writing . . .

William Wordsworth

". . . by yonder Throstle woo'd
That pipes within the Larch-tree, not unseen –
(The Larch, that pushes out in Tassels green
Its bundled Leafits) woo'd to mild Delights
By all the tender Sounds and gentle Sights
Of this sweet Primrose-Month . . ."

Samuel Taylor Coleridge:
from lines sent to William Sotheby

saw and experienced life poetically, but did not compose poetry.

The northern spring advanced by fits and starts with sunshine one day, and snow flurries the next. Then, suddenly, the woods were full of flowers and birds and the cuckoo had arrived – first heard calling in the woods and meadows of Rydal, then at Grasmere, then in Easedale and on the high fells, where William and John heard him when they climbed in the mountains above Langdale and circled Blea Tarn.

The lambs (not born in these parts until the close of April) had by now arrived too. The sunny air echoed to their infant cries and everywhere one looked there were tiny white creatures either lying curled up on the grass, dozing peacefully, nuzzling their mothers, or scampering and dancing with high spirits. The Wordsworths, now feeling themselves in an Arcady truly Miltonic, wandered and wondered in the spirit of *L'Allegro*.

WATER FOWL

Mark how the feathered tenants of the flood,
With grace of motion that might scarcely seem
Inferior to angelical, prolong
Their curious pastime! shaping in mid air
(And sometimes with ambitious wing that soars
High as the level of the mountain-tops)
A circuit ampler than the lake beneath—
Their own domain; but ever, while intent
On tracing and retracing that large round,
Their jubilant activity evolves
Hundreds of curves and circlets, to and fro,
Upward and downward, progress intricate
Yet unperplexed, as if one spirit swayed
Their indefatigable flight. 'Tis done—
Ten times, or more, I fancied it had ceased;
But lo! the vanished company again
Ascending; they approach—I hear their wings,
Faint, faint at first; and then an eager sound,
Past in a moment—and as faint again!
They tempt the sun to sport amid their plumes;
They tempt the water, or the gleaming ice,
To show them a fair image; 'tis themselves,
Their own fair forms, upon the glimmering plain,
Painted more soft and fair as they descend
Almost to touch;—then up again aloft,
Up with a sally and a flash of speed,
As if they scorned both resting-place and rest!

William Wordsworth

DOROTHY WORDSWORTH had a great love of flowers, as her "Journals" testify; she knew many of their names, though not all. For May 16th, 1800, she wrote of her morning's walk round Grasmere, "The woods extremely beautiful . . . I carried a basket for mosses and gathered some wild plants. Oh! that we had a book of botany. All flowers now are gay and deliciously sweet." As time passed, her orchard garden at Dove Cottage produced its own harvest of flowers, "The orchard is full of fox-gloves."

BLEA TARN

(excerpt from "The Excursion" Book II; The Solitary)

. . .We scaled without a track to ease our steps,
A steep ascent; and reached a dreary plain,
With a tumultuous waste of huge hill tops
Before us; savage region! which I paced

Dispirited: when, all at once, behold!
Beneath our feet, a little lowly vale,
A lowly vale, and yet uplifted high
Among the mountains; even as if the spot
Had been from eldest time by wish of theirs
So placed, to be shut out from all the world!
Urn-like it was in shape, deep as an urn;
With rocks encompassed, save that to the south
Was one small opening, where a heathclad ridge

Supplied a boundary less abrupt and close;
A quiet treeless nook, with two green fields,
A liquid pool that glittered in the sun,
And one bare dwelling; one abode, no more!
It seemed the home of poverty and toil,
Though not of want: the little fields, made green
By husbandry of many thrifty years,
Paid cheerful tribute to the moorland house.
—There crows the cock, single in his domain:

The small birds find in spring no thicket there
To shroud them; only from the neighbouring vales
The cuckoo, straggling up to the hill tops,
Shouteth faint tidings of some gladder place.

William Wordsworth

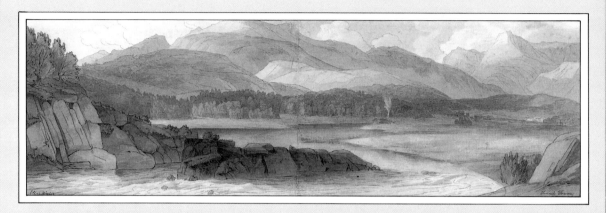

TO THE CUCKOO

O blithe New-comer! I have heard,
I hear thee and rejoice.
O Cuckoo! shall I call thee Bird,
Or but a wandering Voice?

While I am lying on the grass
Thy twofold shout I hear,
From hill to hill it seems to pass
At once far off, and near.

Though babbling only to the Vale,
Of sunshine and of flowers,
Thou bringest unto me a tale
Of visionary hours.

Thrice welcome, darling of the Spring!
Even yet thou art to me
No bird, but an invisible thing,
A voice, a mystery;

The same whom in my schoolboy days
I listened to; that Cry
Which made me look a thousand ways
In bush, and tree, and sky.

To seek thee did I often rove
Through woods and on the green;
And thou wert still a hope, a love;
Still longed for, never seen.

And I can listen to thee yet;
Can lie upon the plain
And listen, till I do beget
That golden time again.

O Blessèd Bird! the earth we pace
Again appears to be
An unsubstantial, faery place;
That is fit home for Thee!

William Wordsworth

AN 'OFFCOME' FROM THE SOUTH

Coleridge had arrived for a stay at Dove Cottage on April 6th, remaining for a month, partly to work with Wordsworth on a new and enlarged edition of *Lyrical Ballads* and partly to inspect the house, to be named Greta Hall, being built at Keswick which he and Wordsworth had earlier noted as a possible home for the Coleridges – perhaps to be shared, later, with William and Dorothy. Greta Hall was being built by William Jackson, a highly successful carrier in the region, whose business had so prospered that he had been able to retire and invest in Greta Hall. It was really two houses in one: the front portion being a "gentleman's residence" with ravishing views; while the less impressive accommodation at the rear of the house was intended for Jackson himself and his

ENTRY AFTER ENTRY in Dorothy's "Journal" describes wandering in Easedale with William and Coleridge. "A fine mild morning – we walked into Easedale. The sun shone. The waters were high, for there had been a great quantity of rain in the night. I . . . sate upon the grass till they came from the waterfall. I saw them there, and heard Wm. flinging stones into the river, whose roaring was loud even where I was", reads one typical entry. The waterfall, Churnmilk Force, may be seen clearly in this photograph.

"JACKSON'S HOUSE", in other words the rear half of Greta Hall, perched on the southern bank of the River Greta. Sir George and Lady Beaumont, for several years, during Southey's tenancy of Greta Hall, rented "Jackson's House" annually for the Keswick "season".

housekeeper, Mrs. Wilson. The front house was a jerrybuilt affair, erected at top speed to cash-in on Keswick's Picturesque explosion, Mr Jackson's intention being to attract as tenant some wealthy and unwary "offcome" (as Cumbrians call folk from the outside world) who would not notice that the windows commanding the sublime vistas also faced the prevailing winds, nor that the house was not built to exclude draughts. Coleridge and the Wordsworths fell headlong for the views, particularly that from the large L-shaped first-floor front room (designed by Jackson to be an elegant drawing-room – he had even installed an harmonium) which Coleridge pounced upon with joy as his study.

PASTORAL

(from "L'Allegro")

Sometime walking, not unseen,
By hedgerow elms, on hillocks green,
Right against the eastern gate
Where the great Sun begins his state,
Robed in flames and amber light,
The clouds in thousand liveries dight;
While the ploughman, near at hand,
Whistles o'er the furrowed land,
And the milkmaid singeth blithe,
And the mower whets his scythe,
And every shepherd tells his tale
Under the hawthorn in the dale.

John Milton

The business of his visit successfully accomplished, Coleridge returned South, to persuade his wife to agree to a move which would distance her three hundred miles from her family and all her friends, "Mighty and numerous objections!" as she expressed it. Meanwhile the Wordsworths enjoyed a heavenly midsummer of long hot days spent sailing on the lake in William's boat, gardening, fishing, or simply idling.

The nights of silvery northern gloaming slipped into dawn almost without any intervening darkness. There was also society if and when the Wordsworths wished for it, albeit of a simple sort. Aggie and John Fisher (Molly's brother and sister-in-law), who lived at Sykeside, a cottage just across the road from Dove Cottage, would drop in for a neighbourly crack (as they called a chat and a joke); or Dorothy would saunter up to High Broadrain, just below the Grasmere foot of Dunmail Raise, to drink tea (then always an

evening ceremony) with the Reverend Joseph Simpson, vicar of Wythburn, and his daughter Peggy; or the Simpsons would stroll down to Dove Cottage, sometimes bringing visiting relatives or friends to meet the Wordsworths.

THE DARKER SIDE OF ARCADY

Though the Lake Country seemed a haven of security and peace the outside world was torn by war and there was, as John Fisher remarked to Dorothy, much "alteration in the times", bringing in its train poverty and hardship for many working people. "He observed that in a short time there would be only two ranks of people, the very rich and the very poor, for those who have small estates says he are forced to sell," noted Dorothy in her *Journal* for May 18th (1800). This general unrest and upheaval was mirrored in the large numbers of beggars and vagrants and "travellers" of all kinds who were constantly passing through the

BEGGARS

She had a tall man's height or more;
Her face from summer's noontide heat
No bonnet shaded, but she wore
A mantle, to her very feet
Descending with a graceful flow,
And on her head a cap as white as new-fallen snow.

Her skin was of Egyptian brown:
Haughty, as if her eye had seen
Its own light to a distance thrown,
She towered, fit person for a Queen
To lead those ancient Amazonian files;
Or ruling Bandit's wife among the Grecian isles.

Advancing, forth she stretched her hand
And begged an alms with doleful plea
That ceased not; on our English land
Such woes, I knew, could never be;
And yet a boon I gave her, for the creature
Was beautiful to see—a weed of glorious feature.

I left her, and pursued my way;
And soon before me did espy
A pair of little Boys at play,
Chasing a crimson butterfly;
The taller followed with his hat in hand,
Wreathed round with yellow flowers the gayest of the land.

The other wore a rimless crown
With leaves of laurel stuck about;
And while both followed up and down,
Each whooping with a merry shout,
In their fraternal features I could trace
Unquestionable lines of that wild Suppliant's face.

Yet *they*, so blithe of heart, seemed fit
For finest tasks of earth or air:
Wings let them have, and they might flit
Precursors to Aurora's car,
Scattering fresh flowers; though happier far, I ween,
To hunt their fluttering game o'er rock and level green.

They dart across my path—but lo,
Each ready with a plaintive whine!
Said I, 'not half an hour ago
Your Mother has had alms of mine.'
'That cannot be,' one answered — 'she is dead:' —
I looked reproof—they saw—but neither hung his head.

'She has been dead, Sir, many a day,'—
'Hush, boys! you're telling me a lie;
It was your Mother, as I say!'
And in the twinkling of an eye,
'Come! come!' cried one, and without more ado
Off to some other play the joyous Vagrants flew!

William Wordsworth

THE SUN HAS LONG BEEN SET

The sun has long been set,
    The stars are out by twos and threes,
The little birds are piping yet
    Among the bushes and trees;
There's a cuckoo, and one or two thrushes,
And a far-off wind that rushes,
And a sound of water that gushes,
And the cuckoo's sovereign cry
Fills all the hollow of the sky.
    Who would go 'parading'
In London, and 'masquerading,'
On such a night of June
With that beautiful soft half-moon,
And all these innocent blisses?
On such a night as this is!

William Wordsworth

valleys, asking for alms as they went. Dorothy's *Journals* give us vivid accounts of these people. One such entry reads,

On Tuesday, May 27th, a very tall woman, tall much beyond the measure of tall women, called at the door. She had on a very long brown cloak, and a very white cap without Bonnet – her face was excessively brown, but it had plainly once been fair. She led a little bare-footed child about 2 years old by the hand and said her husband who was a tinker was gone before with the other children. I gave her a piece of Bread. Afterwards on my road to Ambleside, beside the Bridge at Rydale, I saw her husband sitting by the roadside, his two asses feeding beside him and the two young children at play upon the grass. The man did not beg. I passed on and about ¼ of a mile further I saw two boys before me, one about 10 the other about 8 years old at play chasing a butterfly. They were wild figures, not very ragged, but without shoes and stockings; the hat of the elder was wreathed round with yellow flowers, the younger whose hat was only a rimless crown, had stuck it round with laurel leaves. They continued at play till I drew very near and then they addressed me with the Beggars' cant and the whining voice of sorrow. I said I served your mother this morning. (The Boys were so like the woman who had called at the door that I could not be mistaken.) O! says the elder you could not serve my mother for she's dead and my father's on at the next town – he's a potter. I persisted in my assertion and that I would give them nothing. Says the elder Come, let's away, and away they flew like lightning . . . On my return through Ambleside I met in the street the mother driving her asses; in the two Panniers of one of which were the two little children whom she was chiding and threatening with a wand which she used to drive on her asses, while the little things hung in wantonness over the Pannier's edge. The woman had told me in the morning that she was of Scotland, which her accent fully proved, but that she had lived (I think at Wigton), that they could not keep a house and so they travelled.

On another occasion, when a woman and her little boy, sadly thin and pale, came to the door begging, Dorothy reflected, after they had gone, "Poor creatures! . . . I could not help thinking that we are not half thankful enough that we are placed in that condition of life in which we are. We do not so often bless god for this as we wish for this 50£ that 100£ etc. etc. . . This woman's was but a *common* case."

In mid June the weather turned hot and William and John did much fishing for pike. Dorothy accompanied them on the water in William's boat, or rambled on the shore and lay under the trees. In the evenings they sauntered, enjoying the gloaming and the cuckoo, who continued shouting his head off until it was well past ten o'clock and almost dark.

NEW TENANTS AT GRETA HALL

On Sunday June 29th Coleridge arrived at Dove Cottage together with his wife and four-year-old Hartley. They had come to stay for a few days before crossing the Raise to Keswick and their new home. Paradise would now be complete! Coleridge was instantly taken for a sail on the lake. Unfortunately, he had caught a severe cold on the journey North and, the sail accomplished and appropriate rapture expressed, he retired to bed with a threatened rheumatic fever and remained in bed for the better part of the ensuing week, dosing himself heavily with laudanum. He and his family remained at Dove Cottage for a further fortnight while he recuperated. On July 23rd he left for Greta Hall and Sara and Hartley followed next day.

Sara Coleridge, now philosophically resigned to the parting from her mother, sisters and wide circle of pleasant Bristol friends, settled into her new home. Indeed, "We are most delightfully situated, we have a large and very convenient house furnished with every article of comfort (but without elegance) and we are to pay a very moderate rent," she reported to her sister-in-law, Mrs George Coleridge. She added that they had some very pleasant neighbours in the locality, upon whom Samuel had been calling, but for herself, "My present situation precludes me from

accompanying him as I look every day for an addition to the family and do not chuse to exhibit my figure before strangers."

The expected child would be her third; the second Coleridge child, a boy named Berkeley, had died of smallpox at the age of ten months during his father's absence in Germany; a harrowing experience for Sara from which she had taken some time to recover. However domestic bliss had now been recaptured. Sara, between unpacking boxes and trunks and rearranging the furniture to her own satisfaction gazed from the parlour window at glimpses of shining lakes and sun-bathed mountains, while her husband sat perched high on the leads of

Looking across Derwent Water towards the Newlands Fells, Coleridge's "camp of giant's tents". Causey Pike to the right of the view, Newlands Vale in the centre, leading towards Robinson, with the Buttermere fells in the background; Catbells to the left of the picture, with Hindscarth peeping over. This is virtually the view from Coleridge's study window.

AN EXUBERANT EXPLORER

Before many days had passed Coleridge had abandoned his lofty viewpoint and was exploring the fantastic mountains and giants' tents with an enthusiasm which mounted daily. A letter sent to his friend Francis Wrangham vividly depicts his mood: "My glass being opposite the Window, I seldom shave without cutting myself. Some Mountain or Peak is rising out of the Mist, or some slanting Column of misty Sunlight is sailing across me / so that I offer up soap & blood daily, as an Eye-servant of the Goddess Nature." Breakfast hastily eaten, out he would run, to spend the rest of the day "leaping, bounding and flashing over the tops" (his own description of his abandoned progress).

The first mountain up which he joyously raced was Skiddaw himself; a "mighty monarch" as the Picturesque tourists awesomely called him, and which the said tourists invariably ascended on horseback, accompanied by a guide. The Reverend Sydney Smith, founder of the celebrated *Edinburgh Review*, has left an account of one such ascent, made when he was tutor to young Michael Hicks-Beach and accompanying him on a tour of the North: "Off we set, Michael, the guide and myself, at one in the morning [the object of this decidedly early start being to see the sun rise]. I, who find it rather difficult to stick upon my horse on the plainest roads, did not find that facility increased by the darkness of the morning or the precipitous paths we had to ascend. I made no manner of doubt but that I should roll down into the town of Keswick . . . and be picked up by the town beadle dead in a gutter; moreover I was moved a little for my reputation, for as I had a bottle of brandy in my pocket, placed there by the special exhortations of the guide and landlord, the Keswick coroner and jury would infallibly have brought me in *a Parson as died of drinking.* However, onward we moved, and arrived at the summit. The thermometer stood at 40, the wind was bitter, and the summit totally enveloped in thick clouds, which nearly wetted us through and totally cut off all view of the

the house, sending breathlessly ecstatic scenic descriptions to his friends: "Here I am with Skiddaw at my back; the Lake of Bassenthwaite . . . on my right hand; on my left, and stretching far away into the fantastic mountains of Borrowdale, the Lake of Derwentwater; straight before me a whole camp of giant's tents." These were the Newlands fells.

SUNRISE FROM SKIDDAW: "The wind now puffed away the vapours . . . and gave us a hasty view . . . of the magnificent scene which surrounded us . . . beneath us was Keswick, all quiet, and the solemn tranquil lake of Derwent." Sydney Smith.

sun and the earth, too. Here we regaled upon biscuit and brandy, and waited for the dissipation of the vapor. The guide seemed to be about as much affected by the weather as Skiddaw itself, which mountain in height and brownness of complexion he something resembled . . . The wind now puffed away the vapors at intervals and gave us a hasty view on different quarters of the magnificent scene which surrounded us . . . Beneath us was Keswick, all quiet, and the solemn tranquil lake of Derwent – beyond these the Westmoreland mountains began to be tinged with the golden morning, or we caught the Isle of Man, the northern coast of Ireland, the Frith of Solway, or the hills of Cheviot well known to song and history . . . And so we went down – and Michael grew warm and eat a mounstrous breakfast, and was right pleased with his excursion, and all was well."

It was no coincidence that the guidebooks of the day described the Lake Country as "the British Switzerland!" An ascent of Skiddaw carried distinctly Alpine nuances for these tourists. And indeed Sydney

Smith is restrained, when in comparison with novelist Mrs Radcliffe, who, though her ascent was made in broad daylight, compensated by an excess of hyperbole: "Having engaged a guide, and with horses accustomed to the labour, we began to ascend this tremendous mountain . . . The horses carefully picked their steps along the narrow precipice . . . Sometimes we looked into tremendous chasms, where the torrent fell from ledge to ledge, foaming and shining amidst the dark rock. These streams are

FACE TO FACE WITH THE SUBLIME: a pair of Picturesque Tourists, possibly honeymooners, on their way up Langdale; she on horseback, he on foot at her side. They seem to be chattering happily; no doubt in raptures over the view – Harrison's Stickle springing up ahead of them; cascades pouring down from Stickle Tarn, hidden below Pavey Ark. Hyperbole was a strong characteristic of the Sublime – here Langdale's leading pike rivals the Matterhorn!

"THE VALE OF NEWLANDS silent, & bright . . . What is it that makes the silent bright of the Morning vale so different from that other silence & bright gleam of late evening?" Coleridge notebook entry, August 26th, 1800.

sublime . . . hurrying the sight with them into the abyss, to act, as it were, in sympathy upon the nerves, and to save ourselves from following, we recoil from the view with involuntary horror . . . The hill rose so closely above the precipice as scarcely to allow a ledge wide enough for a single horse. We followed the guide in silence, and till we regained the more open wild, had no leisure for exclamation. It was dreadful to look down."

Coleridge quickly discovered the ridiculous discrepancy between the exaggerated awe with which the Picturesque Tourists treated the hills and the confident manner in which the dalesfolk themselves lived their daily lives in these reputedly hair-raising regions. Shepherds gathered their sheep upon the highest and roughest ground, as had their forefathers before them. Except in the very worst of snowy weather the high passes were regularly crossed at all seasons of the year. For the dalesman, securely at home in the land of his ancestors, the region held few of the terrors which sent shudders down the tourists' spines.

Thus Coleridge had pelted up and down Skiddaw in no time; he took his wife for evening strolls upon its flanks; little Hartley diverted himself by sliding down the grassy slopes, an exercise he thought "the finest sport in the world." An entry in Coleridge's notebook, for Sunday evening, August 24th, reads, "Walked to Lattrigg with Sara and Hartley – the Sun set with slant columns of misty light slanted from him / the light a bright Buff – / Walla Crag purple red, the lake a deep dingy purple blue . . . As we turned round on our return, we see a moving pillar of clouds, flame & smoke, rising, bending, arching, and in swift motion – from what God's chimney doth it issue? – I scarcely ever saw in the sky such variety of shapes, & colors, & colors floating over colors. – Solemnly now lie the black masses on the blue firmament of – not quite night – for still at the foot of Bassenthwaite there is a smoky russet Light. – Tis 9 o'clock."

A POETRY IN THE LANDSCAPE

At the end of August he set off alone to explore Saddleback, ascending by Blease Fell, clambering up to Knowe Crags from whence he skirted round and above the great amphitheatre of precipices and ridges. Over the tops of Gategill, Hallsfell and Doddick he went, dropping down northwards to Scales tarn, "A round bason of vast depth, the west arc an almost perpendic precipice of naked shelving crags (each crag a precipice with a small shelf) – no noise but that of the loose stones rolling away from the feet of the Sheep, that move slowly along these perilous ledges."

His poet's eye took it all in: big dramatic sweeps; small, intriguing details; "The shadow of the Northern wall of the Bason, Green with huge scars of bare blue stone dust, & whiter stones . . . North west between a narrow chasm a little sike wound down . . . at every fall the water fell off in little liquid Icicles, from the points of Moss Jelly bags."

This Saddleback day was followed by a sequence of solitary roamings in the mountains. Immensely more athletic in his youth and prime than Wordsworth, Coleridge sped over the tops in the style of a modern fell runner although his progress was punctuated by pauses for looking, and jotting notes of what he observed. His notebooks increasingly reveal a technique of writing which simultaneously and exactly recorded impressions of scenery and natural objects as they greeted his eye. He was training himself to see shapes, lights, textures and to put down, truly, what he saw. He roamed daily and incessantly upon the fells, analysing sunsets, mists and storm clouds, lights viewed over the lake.

"Wednesday, [August] 26. Morning – six o'clock – Clouds in motion half down Skiddaw, capping & veiling Wanthwaite. No sun, no absolute gleam / but the mountains in & beyond Borrodale were bright & *washed* – And the vale of Newlands silent, & bright – All the crags that enbason the Derwent Water very dark – especially Walla Crag, the crag such a very gloomy purple, its treeage such a very black green – shortly after, the Castle & Grange became illumined – but all soon darkened – a mere gloom of cloudiness. N.B. What is it that makes the silent *bright* of the Morning vale so different from that other silence & bright gleams of late evening? Is it in the mind or is there any physical cause?"

And next day, August 27th, he is still engrossed in observation, notebook at the ready: "A morning of masses of clouds rolling in Sunshine; the Grange well lighted up –. It rained a trifle.

"Sunset lights slanted Newland Hollows – smoke flame over Wanthwaite & under that mass a *wedge* of light on the cliff – but soon the whole of Wanthwaite drunk with a black-hued *scarlet* – the distances of Borrodale duskily colored long after the set, & the end of the Lake crimsoned during the Sunset.

"As I sate on the side of Skiddaw at one o'clock in the noon of this day saw the shore of the Lake & those of its island hemmed with silver in the misty, cloudy, rain-spatter'd Lake."

Eleven o'clock that night found him (slightly under the influence of brandy or laudanum, it is not clear which) contemplating his study fire: "That Volcano of coal, half an inch high, ejaculating its inverted cone of smoke – the smoke in what a furious wind, this way, that way – & what a noise!

> The poet's eye in his tipsy hour
> Hath a magnifying power
> Or rather his soul emancipates his eyes
> Of the accidents of size /
> In unctĩous cones of kindling Coal
> Or smoke from his Pipe's bowl
> His eye can see
> Phantoms of sublimity."

THE BIRTH OF A FRESH TECHNIQUE

This combination of a painter's analytical eye with a poet's apperceptions resulted in his developing a technique of writing Impressionistic in its effect, far in advance of its time: the assemblage, through intent observation, of a series of distinct strokes (each suggesting different possibilities to the intellect) by which a vivid impression of an entirety is achieved. A

much later poet has called this "The optics of holism", but it was defined by Coleridge in a plainly sober notebook entry, thus, "Every one of these [details] is *known* by the Intellect to have a strict & necessary action & reaction on all the rest, & that the whole is made up of parts, each part referring at once

to each & to the whole," and adding, "Nothing more administers to the Picturesque than this phantom of complete visual wholeness in an object, which visually does not form a whole, by the influence *ab intra* of the sense of its perfect Intellectual Beauty or Wholeness."

Melting snow on the ice on Derwent Water from Coleridge's favourite look-out point: Surprise View. One of the strange and unfamiliar visions of the kind that inspired the poet in his "looking and seeing".

Wordsworth, too, had worked at this *pointillist* method of composing; poems such as *Animal Tranquillity and Decay, The Old Cumberland Beggar,* and *A Night Piece* all use this technique. In this last poem he simply gives the various sights and sounds of a clear January night with a full moon in the sky: to the viewer, or the reader, is left the creative mental process of arranging the component parts into a satisfying intellectual, or imaginative whole which is the essence of contemplation: "That inward eye which is the bliss of solitude."

So we have the moon, the wind, the night,

There in a black-blue vault she sails along,
Followed by multitudes of stars, that, small
And sharp, and bright, along the dark abyss
Drive as she drives; how fast they wheel away,
Yet vanish not: – the wind is in the tree,
But they are silent; – still they roll along
Immeasurably distant; and the vault,
Built round by those white clouds, enormous clouds,
Still deepens its unfathomable depth.

"A Night Piece"

The mastery of this technique was a vital step in the development of Wordsworth's remarkable ability to

handle what cinema calls *montage*, used to such miraculous effect in *Michael* and *The Prelude*.

The Lake Country, with its endless interplay of light and scenery stimulated writers – and painters – to this kind of experimentation. Turner, for instance, in the studies of clouds, vapours and skies in his "Colour Beginnings" was working out variations on this same basic theme. In 1799, Farington wrote that, "Turner has no settled process but drives the colours about till he has expressed the Idea in his mind" – or, more correctly, until the colours spontaneously composed an idea, or made a statement.

A UNION OF ORIGINAL MINDS

Looking, and seeing, and analysing how he looked and what he saw was for Wordsworth, as for Coleridge, a vital function within the context of poetry. Throughout their time together in the Lakes the two shared many remarkable moments of visual experience, as Coleridge repeatedly tells us in his notebooks. One such entry tells how he and Wordsworth saw Grasmere from a short distance up Silver Howe, on a winter's morning of thaw: "Half the Lake bright, the other half breezey-dull / the snowy-zebraed Mountain in the *reflection*, all bright / – the Gap between Seat Sandal and Fairfield a beautiful upright blue *Triangle* in the water with, as I thought six or seven slips of Clouds most beautifully coloured & as beautifully disposed / I looked at the Gap itself, & could not perceive any corresponding clouds – noticed it to William, who immediately discovered & made me perceive that they were not clouds, but flakes of Ice on the hither shore close by – instantly the distance altered, & I saw the slips as flakes of Ice close on the surface of the hither shore / yet by volition could again make them clouds."

Today we are so accustomed to the twentieth century techniques of writing and painting that we have forgotten how great a debt art and literature in our era owe to Coleridge and the innovatory work that he, together with Wordsworth, accomplished in the Lakes. And to Dorothy Wordsworth too, who was producing some remarkable writing in her *Journals*, similarly based upon looking and seeing. Here is her portrayal of a birch tree on a windy day,

"It was yielding to the gusty wind with all its tender twigs, the sun shone upon it and it glanced in the wind like a flying sunshiny shower. It was a tree in shape with stem and branches but it was like a Spirit of water . . .The other Birch trees that were near it looked bright and cheerful, but it was a creature by its own self among them."

And here is Coleridge, also concerning himself with birches; on Raven Crag, Thirlmere, reflected in the lake one October morning, "The Reflection of Raven Crag, which at every bestirring the mirror by

DERWENT WATER in a storm: "The dazzling Silver of the Lake in this cloudy, sunny, misty, howling weather!" Coleridge notebook entry for October 21st, 1800.

CLOUD OVER CATBELLS: "Many a walk in the clouds on the mountains did I take." Coleridge describing his struggles with "Christabel" in a letter to Josiah Wedgwood.

gentle motion became a perfect vast Castle Tower, the corners rounded & pillar'd and fluted . . . All this in bright lightest yellow, yellow-green, green, crimson and orange! – The single Birch Trees hung like Tresses of Sea Weed – the Cliffs like organ pipes! and when a little Breath of Air spread a delicious Network over the Lake, all these colours seemed then to float on, like the reflections of the rising or setting Sun."

THE SEARCH FOR INSPIRATION

As Coleridge developed his powers of prose, his power of writing verse seemed to be on the wane. "My poor Muse has deserted me," he had written to Thomas Poole, from Germany, "perhaps when I return to England I may find her again." She continued, however, to elude him. *Christabel* still lay in his desk unfinished; Coleridge had promised to complete the poem for inclusion in the new edition of *Lyrical Ballads*, but the result was intense, exhausting, and frustrated struggle. "I tried and tried, & nothing would come of it . . . many a walk in the clouds on the mountains did I take: but all would not do," he told his patron, Josiah Wedgwood, despairingly. Coleridge had counted upon the euphoric effect of the Lakes to restore his Muse to him, but to no avail. When,

suddenly, she did return, it was as a result of an evening's wining and dining with a local clergyman. Muses are proverbially unpredictable! Clearly this one preferred a libation of wine to a wander in the clouds. *Christabel* Part II, a miraculous performance, was at last composed and, on October 4th in triumph, with a draft of the poem in his pocket, Coleridge set out for Dove Cottage, via Helvellyn, to read *Christabel* to the Wordsworths.

Coleridge had started out late and his walk was a long one, but it was a clear night and the moon was almost at the full. His notes, jotted by moonlight, indicate that by the time he had arrived on the summit of Helvellyn he was virtually in a state of intoxication from the excitement and breathtaking beauty of the walk. Above all he was overawed by moonlit Striding Edge, "That prodigious Precipice of grey stone with deep Wrinkles facing me." He stood for a long time gazing at the astounding scene around him; mountains, lakes, tarns, spread out under the night sky around him, an incredible chiaroscuro of shadow and moonshine.

THE DRAMATIC STRIDING EDGE on Helvellyn, taken from the spot where Coleridge stood gazing at it in awe and wonder.

He arrived at Dove Cottage at eleven o'clock; William and John Wordsworth had gone to bed, but Dorothy was lingering in the garden, enjoying the moon. On hearing Coleridge's voice William came down in his dressing-gown. Coleridge gave a vivid account of his walk over Helvellyn and then read the draft of *Christabel* Part II, with which the Wordsworths were enchanted. He spent the next two days at Grasmere. They bathed in the lake; hunted waterfalls with Dorothy; Wordsworth read his latest poems; and there was an expedition to Stickle Tarn in Langdale. On the third day Coleridge returned to Greta Hall, there to complete *Christabel*, or such was his intention, but could not resist an exploration of the Coledale Fells and Causey Pike, so invitingly spread out before his windows. He made this walk on September 9th: "A heavenly walk . . . lovely!"

LOUISA
AFTER ACCOMPANYING HER
ON A MOUNTAIN EXCURSION

I met Louisa in the shade,
And, having seen that lovely Maid,
Why should I fear to say
That, nymph-like, she is fleet and strong,
And down the rocks can leap along
Like rivulets in May?

And she hath smiles to earth unknown;
Smiles, that with motion of their own
Do spread, and sink, and rise;
That come and go with endless play,
And ever, as they pass away,
Are hidden in her eyes.

She loves her fire, her cottage-home;
Yet o'er the moorland will she roam
In weather rough and bleak;
And, when against the wind she strains,
Oh! might I kiss the mountain rains
That sparkle on her cheek.

Take all that's mine 'beneath the moon,'
If I with her but half a noon
May sit beneath the walls
Of some old cave, or mossy nook,
When up she winds along the brook
To hunt the waterfalls.

William Wordsworth

ANIMAL TRANQUILLITY AND DECAY

A Sketch

The little hedge-row birds
That peck along the road, regard him not.
He travels on, and in his face, his step,
His gait, is one expression; every limb,
His look and bending figure, all bespeak
A man who does not move with pain, but moves
With thought. He is insensibly subdued
To settled quiet: he is one by whom
All effort seems forgotten; one to whom
Long patience hath such mild composure given,
That patience now doth seem a thing of which
He hath no need. He is by nature led
To peace so perfect, that the young behold
With envy, what the old man hardly feels.
I asked him whither he was bound, and what
The object of his journey: he replied
That he was going many miles to take
A last leave of his son, a mariner,
Who from a sea-fight had been brought to
        Falmouth,
And there was dying in an hospital.

William Wordsworth

THE FIR-GROVE

When, to the attractions of the busy world
Preferring studious leisure, I had chosen
A habitation in this peaceful Vale,
Sharp season followed of continual storm
In deepest winter; and, from week to week,
Pathway, and lane, and public road, were clogged
With frequent showers of snow. Upon a hill,
At a short distance from my cottage, stands
A stately Fir-grove, whither I was wont
To hasten, for I found, beneath the roof
Of that perennial shade, a cloistral place
Of refuge, with an unincumbered floor.
Here, in safe covert, on the shallow snow,
And, sometimes, on a speck of visible earth,
The redbreast near me hopped; nor was I loth
To sympathize with vulgar coppice birds
That, for protection from the nipping blast,
Hither repaired.—A single beech-tree grew
Within this grove of firs! and, on the fork
Of that one beech, appeared a thrush's nest;
A last year's nest, conspicuously built
At such small elevation from the ground
As gave sure sign that they, who in that house
Of nature and of love had made their home
Amid the fir-trees, all the summer long
Dwelt in a tranquil spot. And oftentimes
A few sheep, stragglers from some mountain-flock,
Would watch my motions with suspicious stare,
From the remotest outskirts of the grove,—
Some nook where they had made their final stand,
Huddling together from two fears—the fear
Of me and of the storm. Full many an hour
Here did I lose. But in this grove the trees
Had been so thickly planted, and had thriven
In such perplexed and intricate array,
That vainly did I seek, beneath their stems
A length of open space, where to and fro
My feet might move without concern or care;
And, baffled thus, though earth from day to day
Was fettered, and the air by storm disturbed,
I ceased the shelter to frequent,—and prized,
Less than I wished to prize, that calm recess.

   The snows dissolved, and genial Spring returned
To clothe the fields with verdure. Other haunts
Meanwhile were mine; till one bright April day,
By chance retiring from the glare of noon
To this forsaken covert, there I found
A hoary pathway traced between the trees,
And winding on with such an easy line
Along a natural opening, that I stood
Much wondering how I could have sought in vain

For what was now so obvious. To abide,
For an allotted interval of ease,
Under my cottage-roof, had gladly come
From the wild sea a cherished Visitant;
And with the sight of this same path—begun,
Begun and ended, in the shady grove,
Pleasant conviction flashed upon my mind
That, to this opportune recess allured,
He had surveyed it with a finer eye,
A heart more wakeful; and had worn the track
By pacing here, unwearied and alone,
In that habitual restlessness of foot
That haunts the Sailor measuring o'er and o'er
His short domain upon the vessel's deck,
While she pursues her course through the dreary sea.

   When thou hadst quitted Esthwaite's pleasant shore,
And taken thy first leave of those green hills
And rocks that were the play-ground of thy youth,
Year followed year, my Brother! and we two,

Conversing not, knew little in what mould
Each other's mind was fashioned; and at length,
When once again we met in Grasmere Vale,
Between us there was little other bond
Than common feelings of fraternal love.
But thou, a School-boy, to the sea hadst carried
Undying recollections; Nature there
Was with thee; she, who loved us both, she still
Was with thee; and even so didst thou become
A *silent* Poet; from the solitude
Of the vast sea didst bring a watchful heart
Still couchant, an inevitable ear,
And an eye practised like a blind man's touch.
—Back to the joyless Ocean thou art gone;
Nor from this vestige of thy musing hours
Could I withhold thy honoured name,—and now
I love the fir-grove with a perfect love.
Thither do I withdraw when cloudless suns
Shine hot, or wind blows troublesome and strong;
And there I sit at evening, when the steep

Of Silver-how, and Grasmere's peaceful lake,
And one green island, gleam between the stems
Of the dark firs, a visionary scene!
And while I gaze upon the spectacle
Of clouded splendour, on this dream-like sight
Of solemn loveliness, I think on thee,
My Brother, and on all which thou has lost.
Nor seldom, if I rightly guess, while Thou,
Muttering the verses which I muttered first
Among the mountains, through the midnight watch
Art pacing thoughtfully the vessel's deck
In some far region, here, while o'er my head,
At every impulse of the moving breeze,
The fir-grove murmurs with a sea-like sound,
Alone I tread this path;—for aught I know,
Timing my steps to thine; and, with a store
Of undistinguishable sympathies,
Mingling most earnest wishes for the day
When we, and others whom we love, shall meet
A second time, in Grasmere's happy Vale.

William Wordsworth

THE IDYLL IS THREATENED

Crisis was now brewing in Paradise.

Not that events seemed to be pointing in that direction, in fact, quite the reverse. To be sure there was a wrench when John Wordsworth was called away from Grasmere to join his long awaited ship, *Abergavenney*, but he assured William and Dorothy that as soon as he had made enough money from his merchant venturing he would retire from the sea and settle with them in Grasmere. Shortly before John's departure a new son had been born to the Coleridges on September 14th. The child, named Derwent, was a large and healthy one and Sara made a rapid recovery – three nights after the birth she was up and dining with Coleridge in the parlour. "There's for you!" he exclaimed exultantly to his friends.

At this stage the marriage was still a successful one. Sara adored her Samuel, and he delighted in Sara, of whom he was very proud. True, she had not proved to be the "meek-eyed Maiden mild" that Southey had promised she would be. Sara didn't in the least resemble her complaisant, rather apathetic sister Edith, but was of a lively, independent, and at times distinctly fiery disposition. Since Coleridge, too, possessed a strong temper when provoked (unless, instead, he fell into silence and the sulks) their marriage was not without episodes of friction. While Sara's temper subsided as rapidly as it boiled up – a purely ephemeral rage – Coleridge, as he himself admitted, rarely could recall what he had said to, or about, people in his worst fits of anger,

"Wholly forgotten, as is commonly the unfortunate case with things said or written in a passion . . . forgotten by the Aggressor & for ever remembered by the Receiver."

Fortunately for him Sara was of an exceptionally magnanimous disposition. To quote her daughter

THE ROCK OF NAMES, by the roadside above old Wythburn Water, on which William, Dorothy, Coleridge, John Wordsworth, and Mary and Sarah Hutchinson carved their initials as a symbolic gesture of fraternity. (It should be noted that Mrs. Coleridge's initials were excluded.) In the 1890's, after the creation of the reservoir at Thirlmere, it was necessary to build a new road and the Rock of Names was irreverently blasted by navvies. Cannon Rawnsley of Crosthwaite attempted to cement the fragments together, but the result was not happy.

Sara, writing of her mother, "Hasty she was at the moments of provocation, but never was anyone more just to all mankind . . . less swayed by peevish resentment." Coleridge, in his "passions", said many bitter things to and about his wife, but once her heated immediate response was over, she bore no grudge. However, at this stage of her life she did resent, understandably, the way in which the Wordsworths, whether consciously or not, attempted to monopolize Coleridge, and to exclude her from their charmed circle: a process which had quickly become established following their arrival at Alfoxden and had steadily intensified.

Baby Derwent caught a chill in the draughty house, shortly following his birth, and developed bronchitis. For several days his life was in danger. Sara feared she would lose him, as she had lost her beloved second son, despite devoted nursing. While she anxiously tended Derwent, returning him to robust health, Coleridge frenziedly attempted to catch up with some of his professional journalism, for which he was contracted to the *Morning Post*, as well as produce manuscripts for publishers who had paid him advances and were now expecting something in return. The removal north had been expensive and the new baby was a further expense. Now alarmingly short of money, Coleridge could not afford to stay away from his desk.

The Wordsworths had seemed delighted with *Christabel* Part II, but within forty-eight hours they were finding reasons why the poem should not be included in *Lyrical Ballads*. This was chiefly because Wordsworth had decided that it was not suited in style or content for the book, but also because he and Dorothy had now tempered their initially great enthusiasm for the poem by an anxiety "to acquit their judgements of any blindness to the very numerous defects," as Coleridge wryly commented. *The Ancient Mariner* had already been subjected to similar disparaging scrutiny by Wordsworth and had been extensively revised by Coleridge as a result.

It is not unknown for poets to behave like prima donnas and Wordsworth throughout his life was prone to do so, but this was the first occasion upon which he had demonstrated his propensity so manifestly to the face of his devoted friend Coleridge. The latter was pathologically sensitive by nature and as a result of this treatment meted out to him by Wordsworth he was flung into a profound depression. Abruptly, he abandoned writing poetry: *Christabel* remained unfinished. He succumbed to a series of rheumatic chills and violent stomach upsets. Each

THE TINY CHURCH of Wythburn stands at the foot of Helvellyn, close to the shore of today's Thirlmere on the route between Grasmere and Keswick. Manchester Waterworks Committee balked at drowning the church, famous for its minute size and because Wordsworth extolled it. Downman shows it here as it was before Victorian "civilizing influences" altered it.

time he showed the slightest improvement in his health he set out in wintry wind and wet to walk the fourteen miles to Grasmere. Each time, not surprisingly, he renewed his rheumatic symptoms, frequently being obliged to return to Keswick in a chaise, too ill to walk.

THE ROAD TO RUIN

As medicine for his illness, and a panacea for his dejection, Coleridge now took immense quantities of opium. He had first become reliant upon the drug as a schoolboy, when he had had rheumatic fever and the doctors had dosed him liberally (and, within the context of medicine of that day and age, perfectly correctly) with laudanum. Since then his addiction to opium had steadily intensified so that now he was poised on the perilous brink of saturation by the drug, and inevitable total disaster.

The heroin addict of today faces virtually certain death within a foreseeably not too distant future. In Coleridge's day morphine, usually taken in the form of laudanum (the alcoholic tincture of opium) was slowly, albeit surely, destructive but this destruction, though deeply distressing in its consequences (ruining health, ruining marital and personal relationships, making steady work and regular gainful employment impossible, in short, completely wrecking the victim) was not necessarily fatal. The morphine habit, once acquired, could not be broken but, in properly

treated cases, might be controlled. Coleridge maintained upon a reasonably even keel by selfless friendship and firm, sympathetic support (such as he had received from Thomas Poole at Nether Stowey), might have travelled down the years resorting to regular, controlled opium, and avoiding outright catastrophe. However, Wordsworth's rejection of him as a poet struck Coleridge a mortal blow which precipitated his calamitous collapse and destruction.

His health crumbled. The large quantities of laudanum and brandy (the latter to keep the opium upon his stomach) which he took undermined his health still further. His condition made it impossible for him to work and he was soon up to his eyes in

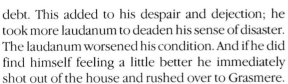

Not all the Coleridge-Wordsworth visiting was one way – the Wordsworths not infrequently went over to Keswick; though they never stayed long because of the cold reception given them by Mrs. Coleridge. The best part of the visit was usually the walk there and back, sometimes via the village of Watenlath, a tiny, highly picturesque hamlet, beside a tarn, lying in a hidden valley between Thirlmere and Borrowdale. The bridge, one of Wordsworth's favourites, with its high arch and low parapets, is a fine example of a medieval wool-pack bridge.

family finances, and the darkness of the future. She began to remonstrate with him, declaring that opium, far from alleviating his sufferings, was clearly contributing to them, and that his habit of racing out into the wind and rain over to Grasmere the moment that his health improved, thereby provoking his rheumatic symptoms and confining him to bed again, was nothing less than insane. She pointed to the bundles of bills, asking Coleridge to consider how they were to live if he were too ill to work and there was not a penny coming into the house, with the exception of the Wedgwood annuity, which was not sufficient for a household such as theirs, with the constant drain of laudanum and brandy. They had reached the point where they could not keep the house warm, and had not enough food for a sustaining diet.

In his heart he knew that Sara was right. He became riddled with guilt and remorse. This in turn bred resentment. What right had she to reproach him, a sick man who needed sympathy above all else? The instant he could struggle from his bed again he hurried away to Dove Cottage, there to pour out complaints about Sara's bad temper and lack of understanding. The Wordsworths, oddly blind to the reality of what was happening at Greta Hall, condoled with him. Invariably he returned home with renewed sickness upon him, fetching a fresh spate of "ill-

debt. This added to his despair and dejection; he took more laudanum to deaden his sense of disaster. The laudanum worsened his condition. And if he did find himself feeling a little better he immediately shot out of the house and rushed over to Grasmere.

Sara became increasingly distraught with anxiety over her husband's health, the desperate state of the tempered speeches" down upon his head. He buried himself deep among his pillows and swallowed more laudanum, more brandy, lashing out at Sara – and Hartley, when the child ventured near him – with a tongue made "wrong and bitter." It was a deeply tragic time at Greta Hall.

The Wordsworths, though perceiving that something had gone very wrong in Paradise, seem not to have entertained the slightest suspicion that they themselves had contributed to the catastrophe, and continued to contribute to it by encouraging Coleridge's complaints about his miserable homelife, thereby driving a wedge between himself and his wife. Of course at this stage they did not realize the full extent of his opium addition, nor did they understand the fearfully destructive nature of this kind of addiction.

Even without Wordsworth's insensitive treatment of him as a poet, Coleridge's poetry would have deserted him. Morphine, although initially a stimulant, when taken to saturation has a deadening effect, fatally destructive to creative impulse. Tragically Coleridge lamented from his sick-bed: "The Poet is dead in me – my imagination . . . lies, like a Cold Snuff on the circular Rim of a Brass Candle-stick, without even a stink of Tallow to remind you that it was once cloathed & mitred with Flame . . . I was once a Volume of Gold Leaf, rising & riding on every breath of Fancy . . . but I have beaten myself back into weight & density, & now I sink in quick silver, yea, remain squat and square on the earth."

THE POETRY OF SHEPHERDS

Almost certainly the chief reason for Wordsworth's tardiness in real understanding of the Coleridge dilemma was that Wordsworth was totally preoccupied by attempting to capture, in his poetry, the essential heart of the Lake Country: what it was truly like to be a native of the place, a shepherd, through whose eyes, ears, actions and daily round of time-honoured tasks and cares, the poet would indeed see into the *life* of things. Though the shepherd poems and passages were composed essentially as a development of the time-honoured romanticized pastoral theme, the close and informed observation that Wordsworth brought to his work resulted in the most accurate portraiture of shepherds at work upon the hills that has ever been achieved. Some idealization of the subject inevitably occurs in this poetry, but the reality of Wordsworth's shepherds and their way of life is utterly true and convincing.

As a boy Wordsworth had spent many winter evenings listening to Dame Tyson telling tales of local lore: some based on occurrences remembered from her own youth; some recollections handed down by word of mouth from one generation to the next, so that it was impossible to determine whether the incident being so vividly recounted, or the legendary character so convincingly delineated, belonged to centuries distant in time, or was of more recent date. Such a man was the shepherd Michael,

In wordsworth's day, sheep were not brought down to the farmsteads for attention as frequently as they are nowadays, but were tended in folds among the fells. Here we see sheep being gathered on Wrynose Fell, near Blea Tarn, for salving; a task which took place in late October, early November. (Dorothy, in a "Journal" entry for November 11th, 1800, a time when William was pre-occupied with composing "Michael", writes, "William had been working at the sheepfold. They were salving sheep".) Salving was an ancient substitute for dipping (which did not come into common usage until the close of the nineteenth century), carried out to destroy ticks and other parasites infesting the sheep's fleece. The salve was traditionally made of stockholm-tar mixed with lard, or cheap foreign butter. The wool was separated in clusters or sheddings, as they are called, and the salve applied to the sheep's skin; before long the warmth of the animal's body made the salve melt and spread over the skin surface.

*I*N THIS SKETCH *of the writer and artist Major Gilpin clipping a sheep, note the traditional clipping shears (still used in Cumbria today by the experts, who insist that a first-rate clip can never be obtained with electric shears!). Also note the traditional clipping stool – again still used today. A good hand-shear clipper may seem to operate in an apparently leisurely manner, but in reality he works at great speed: if he is top-notch he will be a "hundred a day man". The sheep, held across his lap, looks comfortable throughout and emerges as smooth as a lamb.*

Time passed and the boy grew into a youth and was able to relieve his ageing sire of many of the more strenuous tasks of shepherding. But by misfortune Michael, at the age of eighty-four, was summoned to discharge the forfeiture upon a surety undertaken for a nephew. Rather than sell any of their land, Michael and Isabel decided to send Luke to a city kinsman, a thriving tradesman, in the trusting belief that the youth would quickly earn the money necessary to make good his father's loss.

Before Luke departed, Michael, in a moving farewell ceremony, made him lay the cornerstone of a sheepfold in Greenhead Gill, to be built by the patriarch during Luke's absence. This cornerstone was a covenant between father and son that the former, despite his age, would carry on flocks and farmstead until the son returned, and that Luke in the city would resist temptation and, in due course, return to the home and pursuits of his ancestors.

> 'This was a work for us; and now, my son,
> It is a work for me. But, lay one stone –
> Here, lay it for me, Luke, with thine own hands.
> Nay, boy, be of good hope – we both may live
> To see a better day. At eighty-four
> I am still strong and stout; do thou thy part,
> I will do mine. I will begin again
> With many tasks that were resigned to thee;
> Up to the heights, and in among the storms,
> Will I without thee go again, and do
> All works which I was wont to do alone
> Before I knew thy face . . . Lay now the corner-stone,
> As I requested; and hereafter, Luke,
> When thou art gone away, should evil men
> Be thy companions, think of me, my son,
> And of this moment; hither turn thy thoughts,
> And God will strengthen thee . . .'

At first Luke prospered in the city, but the temptations met there were too much for him. He went to the bad and finally had to seek a hiding place overseas, and was lost to his parents.

> There is a comfort in the strength of love;
> 'Twill make a thing endurable, which else
> Would break the heart: old Michael found it so . . .
>   Among the rocks
> He went, and still looked up upon the sun,
> And listened to the wind; and as before
> Performed all kinds of labour for his sheep,
> And for the land his small inheritance.
> And to that hollow dell from time to time
> Did he repair, to build the fold of which

traditionally a Grasmere shepherd of prodigious physique and strength, and natural nobility of nature, married to an industrious and thrifty wife, Isabel. To this pair, late in life, was born a son, Luke, who was reared and trained by his father to carry on the ancestral role of shepherd and yeoman-flockmaster.

His flock had need. 'Tis not forgotten yet
The pity which was then in every heart
For the old man – and 'tis believed by all
That many and many a day he thither went,
And never lifted up a single stone.

That there actually was a shepherd named Michael who had lived in a humble farmstead at the foot of Greenhead Gill with his wife and son and whose story had followed this simple, but deeply moving course, we need not doubt. Such is the reliability of oral tradition among remote peoples. We may even accept that in his final days he might have been seen sitting by the sheepfold, alone apart from his ever faithful and ageing dog lying at his feet, as the last stanza of the poem tells us. It is even a possibility that the poem's two most touching lines,

> . . . many and many a day he thither went,
> And never lifted up a single stone

may have been quoted by Wordsworth direct from Dame Tyson, who may well have received them direct from whoever told her the story, and so back into the recesses of time.

Certainly the tale of Michael so moved and inspired Wordsworth that he made it the theme of his major pastoral poem, one of the great poems in the English language. It is too long to give in its entirety here – four hundred and eighty seven lines in all, and when first projected and being worked upon it was even longer.

EVER-EXPANDING DREAMS

Michael was intended as the pastoral section of the great *magnum opus* Wordsworth was now engaged upon. This was a project suggested to him by Coleridge during the heady days at Stowey: a philosophical poem to be called *The Recluse or Views of Nature, Man and Society*. Its subject matter was to cover mankind's progress from the primitive, through the pastoral and successive states of society up to the "high civilizations of cities and towns", leading to a melancholy picture of contemporary degeneracy and vice, concluding with Man's regeneration and the realization of a Utopia on earth. During the course of the work, Man's philosophical, scientific, historical, political and social knowledge, together with his poetic impulses and achievements, would be scrutinized and synthesized into the poem. "Indeed I know not any thing which will not come within the scope of my plan," Wordsworth had announced buoyantly in 1798, entirely carried away by Coleridge's insistence that "The Giant Wordsworth" (as Coleridge at that time was calling him) and Wordsworth alone was capable of producing this "Great Work . . . of great objects and elevated Conceptions."

The Ruined Cottage, The Old Cumberland Beggar, Michael, The Brothers, Home at Grasmere, and *The Excursion* were among the poems composed with the intention that they would form part of this *magnum opus*, with *The Prelude* as a prologue. Had the work been completed it would have been three times as long as Milton's *Paradise Lost*! The extravagance of size and scope of the work's projected outline was, initially, almost entirely due to Coleridge's flamboyant notions of the possible.

During the period of the first three years or so following the birth of this vast idea, Wordsworth worked in a state of high enthusiasm and confidence, encouraged constantly by Coleridge, who, following his dejected conclusion that he himself could no longer write poetry, saw his future role as mentor to other poets, which really meant mentor to Wordsworth. Wordsworth was not only happy but anxious to have Coleridge constantly at his elbow in that capacity. An astonishing amount of marvellous blank verse, in the shape of poems which could stand upon their own, though all intended for ultimate synthesis in the *The Recluse*, came from Wordsworth in these early years of the attempted project: "To this work I mean to devote the Prime of my life and the chief force of my mind," he declared.

Although *Michael* was, and remained, Wordsworth's major pastoral poem, much other poetry about shepherds found its way into other intended parts of *The Recluse*, including two especially fine passages in the 1805–6 version of *The Prelude*; the second of these passages describes an adventure (originally recounted to Wordsworth by his "household Dame", Ann Tyson), involving a shepherd and his son: clearly Michael and Luke – written for the *Michael* poem but not used, finding its place in the 1805 *Prelude* instead.

> *"Dreamlike the blending also of the whole*
> *Harmonious landscape, all along the shore . . .*
> *And the Clear hills, as high as they ascend*
> *Heavenward, so deep piercing the lake below."*
>
> *William Wordsworth: "Home at Grasmere"*

THE LAKELAND SHEPHERD

(excerpt from "The Prelude" 1805, Book VIII)

Yet, hail to you
Your rocks and precipices! Ye that seize
The heart with firmer grasp! Your snows and streams
Ungovernable, and your terrifying winds,
That howled so dismally when I have been
Companionless among your solitudes!
There, 'tis the shepherd's task the winter long
To wait upon the storms: of their approach
Sagacious, from the height he drives his flock
Down into sheltering coves, and feeds them there
Through the hard time, long as the storm is locked,
(So do they phrase it) bearing from the stalls
A toilsome burden up the craggy ways,
To strew it on the snow. And when the spring
Looks out, and all the mountains dance with lambs,
He through the enclosures won from the steep waste,
And through the lower heights hath gone his rounds;
And when the flock, with warmer weather, climbs
Higher and higher, him his office leads
To range among them, through the hills dispersed,
And watch their goings, whatsoever track
Each wanderer chooses for itself; a work
That lasts the summer through. He quits his home
At day-spring, and no sooner doth the sun
Begin to strike him with a fire-like heat,
Than he lies down upon some shining place,
And breakfasts with his dog. When he hath stayed,
As for the most he doth, beyond his time,
He springs up with a bound, and then away!
Ascending fast with his long pole in hand,

Or winding in and out among the crags.
What need to follow him through what he does
Or sees in his day's march? He feels himself,
In those vast regions where his service is,
A freeman, wedded to his life of hope
And hazard, and hard labour interchanged
With that majestic indolence so dear
To native man. A rambling schoolboy, thus
Have I beheld him, without knowing why
Having felt his presence in his own domain,
As of a lord and master, or a power,
Or genius, under Nature, under God,
Presiding; and severest solitude
Seemed more commanding oft when he was there.
Seeking the raven's nest, and suddenly
Surprised with vapours, or on rainy days
When I have angled up the lonely brooks,

Mine eyes have glanced upon him few steps off,
In size a giant, stalking through the fog,
His sheep like Greenland bears; at other times
When round some shady promontory turning,
His form hath flashed upon me, glorified
By the deep radiance of the setting sun:
Or him have I descried in distant sky,
A solitary object and sublime,
Above all height! like an aerial cross,
As it is stationed on some spiry rock
Of the Chartreuse, for worship. Thus was man
Ennobled outwardly before mine eyes,
And thus my heart at first was introduced
To an unconscious love and reverence
Of human nature.

William Wordsworth

A SHEPHERD'S ADVENTURE

———————

(excerpt from "The Prelude" 1805, VIII)

At the first falling of autumnal snow
A shepherd and his son one day went forth
(Thus did the Matron's tale begin) to seek
A straggler of their flock. They both had ranged
Upon this service the preceding day
All over their own pastures and beyond,
And now at sunrise sallying out again
Renewed their search begun where from Dove Crag,
Ill home for bird so gentle, they looked down
On Deep-dale Head, and Brothers-water, named
From those two brothers that were drowned therein.
Thence, northward, having passed by Arthur's Seat,
To Fairfield's highest summit; on the right
Leaving St Sunday's Pike, to Grisedale Tarn
They shot, and over that cloud-loving hill,
Seat Sandal, a fond lover of the clouds;
Thence up Helvellyn, a superior mount
With prospect underneath of Striding-Edge,
And Grisedale's houseless vale, along the brink
Of Russet Cove, and those two other coves,
Huge skeletons of crags, which from the trunk
Of old Helvellyn spread their arms abroad,
And make a stormy harbour for the winds.
Far went those shepherds in their devious quest,
From mountain ridges peeping as they passed
Down into every glen: at length the boy
Said, 'Father, with your leave I will go back,
And range the ground which we have searched before.'
So speaking, southward down the hill the lad
Sprang like a gust of wind, crying aloud
'I know where I shall find him.' 'For take note,'
Said here my grey-haired Dame, 'that though the storm
Drive one of these poor creatures miles and miles,
If he can crawl he will return again
To his own hills, the spots where, when a lamb,
He learnt to pasture at his mother's side.'
After so long a labour, suddenly
Bethinking him of this, the boy
Pursued his way towards a brook whose course
Was through that unfenced tract of mountain-ground
Which to his father's little farm belonged,
The home and ancient birth-right of their flock.
Down the deep channel of the stream he went,

Prying through every nook; meanwhile the rain
Began to fall upon the mountain tops,
Thick storm and heavy which for three hours' space
Abated not; and all that time the boy
Was busy in his search until at length
He spied the sheep upon a plot of grass,
An island in the brook. It was a place
Remote and deep, piled round with rocks where foot
Of man or beast was seldom used to tread;
But now, when everywhere the summer grass
Had failed, this one adventurer, hunger-pressed,
Had left his fellows, and made his way alone
To the green plot of pasture in the brook.
Before the boy knew well what he had seen
He leapt upon the island with proud heart
And with a prophet's joy. Immediately
The sheep sprang forward to the further shore
And was borne headlong by the roaring flood.
At this the boy looked round him, and his heart
Fainted with fear; thrice did he turn his face
To either brink; nor could he summon up
The courage that was needful to leap back
Cross the tempestuous torrent; so he stood,
A prisoner on the island, not without
More than one thought of death and his last hour.
Meanwhile the father had returned alone
To his own house; and now at the approach
Of evening he went forth to meet his son,
Conjecturing vainly for what cause the boy
Had stayed so long. The shepherd took his way
Up his own mountain grounds, where, as he walked
Along the steep that overhung the brook,
He seemed to hear a voice, which was again
Repeated, like the whistling of a kite.
At this, not knowing why, as oftentimes
Long afterwards he has been heard to say,
Down to the brook he went, and tracked its course
Upwards among the o'erhanging rocks; nor thus
Had he gone far, ere he espied the boy
Where on that little plot of ground he stood
Right in the middle of the roaring stream,
Now stronger every moment and more fierce.
The sight was such as no one could have seen
Without distress and fear. The shepherd heard
The outcry of his son, he stretched his staff
Towards him, bade him leap, which word scarce said,
The boy was safe within his father's arms.

William Wordsworth

COLERIDGE IN DECLINE

The year 1801 was a calamitous one for Coleridge, whose descent into the horrors and pains of full morphine reliance increased at a terrifying pace. One bout of illness after the next continued to engulf him; his debts mounted; his sleep was tormented by nightmares; dejection swamped him. Morphine disturbed his emotional balance; he developed an abrupt, morbid aversion to his wife and, simultaneously, an equally abrupt and morbid infatuation for Miss Sarah Hutchinson (Wordsworth's future sister-in-law) whom he pestered with his attentions, so that she in turn became nervously distressed and melancholy. The Wordsworths, inescapably, were witnesses of this catastrophic decline of the marvellous young genius, "Brother of our hearts", whose arrival in the Lakes they had looked forward to as the ultimate in Arcadian bliss,

> Philosopher and Poet, in whose sight
> These mountains will rejoice in open joy.
> *"Home at Grasmere"*

Now he deluged them incessantly with complaints about his health, complaints about his wife, tales of domestic strife and woe. When he could not stagger over to Grasmere in person, appearing with swollen eyes and smothered in boils, a wreck of his former self, he sent them letters of despair, so that even the patiently ever-sympathetic Dorothy is to be found exclaiming, "Oh, for one letter of perfect uncomplainingness!" But the long recital of affliction continued unabated.

The Wordsworths had yet to realize that morphine was the root cause of his disasters. He himself refused to admit that such was the case and blamed everything upon his wife's ill temper and unloving nature, and the damp Lake Country climate. At last the Wordsworths put it to him that if his health and genius were truly being destroyed by an unhappy marriage then he should seek a separation. This step seemed to Coleridge to be "so awful" that he shrank from it, instead arranging to spend the winter of 1801–2 in London, working in Fleet Street, with the possibility of seeking a warmer climate overseas in the spring.

THE POETRY CONTINUES

With Coleridge in London the Wordsworths were relieved of the sad distraction of his distressful visits and endless flow of complaints. William, released

from this strain, experienced another great surge of creative energy. We find entries in Dorothy's *Journal* for this period: "William highly poetical." He worked upon translations from Chaucer and a long poem, *The Ruined Cottage*, which ultimately became the opening books of *The Excursion*.

Despite his profound attachment to his sister (perhaps because of it) Wordsworth had now made up his mind to marry Mary Hutchinson, a young woman of great sweetness of disposition, and subtle beauty and charm, and a friend of both Dorothy and William since their adolescence. The date for the marriage was at first 1802, but was presently deferred to the autumn; Annette Vallon had to be taken into consideration. The temporary cessation of hostilities between France and England meant that she and Wordsworth were able to correspond again. Neither party had retained the least desire to marry the other, but Wordsworth was the father of Annette's child and so it was arranged that, before his marriage to Mary, he and Dorothy should visit France to see Annette and little Caroline.

Dorothy's *Journal* draws us an intimate portrait of life at Grasmere during this period of strong emotion and great poetry, a portrait not always in accordance with the popular public image of a poet at work. On Friday March 26th (1802) Wordsworth ordered a load of dung (it being beautiful spring weather and just right for gardening) and before going to bed he suddenly composed *The Rainbow*,

> My heart leaps up when I behold
> A rainbow in the sky . . .

lines which served as the introductory theme of the great ode, *Intimations of Immortality*, which he began composing next morning over breakfast. Then the dung arrived and, as Dorothy tells us, "William went to work in the garden", digging it in, while his heart and mind beat with the strophes:

*J*OHN HARDEN'S *sketch of an unidentified man and woman at work on a manuscript: William and Dorothy must have looked much like this when they sat together, by candlelight, working on one of William's manuscripts, as Dorothy describes, for instance, in this "Journal" entry for Friday, February 12th: "After the candles were lighted . . . I almost finished writing "The Pedlar"; but poor William wore himself out with labour . . . Went to bed at 12 o'clock."*

There was a time when meadow, grove and stream,
The earth, and every common sight,
    To me did seem
  Apparelled in celestial light,
The glory and the freshness of a dream.

The next day the Wordsworths went to Keswick for a week's stay, Coleridge having now returned to Greta Hall. There was much walking, talking, party-going and gossip. On the evening before the Wordsworths departed there was a tea-party and Dorothy recited to the company some of William's verses, including lines from his new ode. This prompted Coleridge to compose an ode in reply – the celebrated *Dejection Ode*, the first opium-sodden draft of which took the form of a melancholy letter to Sarah Hutchinson. Revised and polished extensively this ode (now addressed to "Edmund", a soubriquet for Wordsworth) was published in the *Morning Post* on October 4th 1802, Wordsworth's wedding day and the seventh anniversary of Coleridge's own wedding. The final version, given here, which appeared in the publication, *Sibylline Leaves* in 1817, is the one that the world best knows.

Although the *Intimations* ode (not published until 1807) has become one of the best loved and most inspiring poems ever, in its own day and age it never rivalled in popularity Coleridge's *Dejection*, which touched a deep chord in an era devoted to the idea of tormented poetic genius. *Dejection* was exactly to the taste of the early decades of the nineteenth century.

THE RAINBOW

My heart leaps up when I behold
    A rainbow in the sky:
So was it when my life began;
So is it now I am a man;
So be it when I shall grow old,
    Or let me die!
The Child is father of the Man;
And I could wish my days to be
Bound each to each by natural piety.

William Wordsworth

ODE: INTIMATIONS OF IMMORTALITY FROM RECOLLECTIONS OF EARLY CHILDHOOD

The Child is father of the Man;
And I could wish my days to be
Bound each to each by natural piety.

There was a time when meadow, grove, and stream,
The earth, and every common sight,
    To me did seem
    Apparelled in celestial light,
The glory and the freshness of a dream.
It is not now as it hath been of yore;—
    Turn wheresoe'er I may,
    By night or day,
The things which I have seen I now can see no more.

    The Rainbow comes and goes,
    And lovely is the Rose,
    The Moon doth with delight
Look round her when the heavens are bare;
    Waters on a starry night
    Are beautiful and fair;
    The sunshine is a glorious birth;
    But yet I know, where'er I go,
That there hath past away a glory from the earth.

Now, while the birds thus sing a joyous song,
    And while the young lambs bound
        As to the tabor's sound,
To me alone there came a thought of grief:
A timely utterance gave that thought relief,
        And I again am strong:
The cataracts blow their trumpets from the steep;
No more shall grief of mine the season wrong;
I hear the Echoes through the mountains throng,
The Winds come to me from the fields of sleep,
        And all the earth is gay;
            Land and sea
        Give themselves up to jollity,
        And with the heart of May
        Doth every Beast keep holiday;—
            Thou Child of Joy,
Shout round me, let me hear thy shouts, thou happy
                                        Shepherd-boy!

Ye blessèd Creatures, I have heard the call
    Ye to each other make; I see
The heavens laugh with you in your jubilee;
    My heart is at your festival,
        My head hath its coronal,
The fulness of your bliss, I feel—I feel it all.
        Oh evil day! if I were sullen
        While Earth herself is adorning,
        This sweet May-morning,

And the Children are culling
  On every side,
In a thousand valleys far and wide,
Fresh flowers; while the sun shines warm,
And the Babe leaps up on his Mother's arm:—
  I hear, I hear, with joy I hear!
  —But there's a Tree, of many, one,
A single Field which I have looked upon,
Both of them speak of something that is gone:
  The Pansy at my feet
  Doth the same tale repeat:
Whither is fled the visionary gleam?
Where is it now, the glory and the dream?

Our birth is but a sleep and a forgetting:
The Soul that rises with us, our life's Star,
  Hath had elsewhere its setting,
    And cometh from afar:
  Not in entire forgetfulness,
  And not in utter nakedness,
But trailing clouds of glory do we come
  From God, who is our home:
Heaven lies about us in our infancy!
Shades of the prison-house begin to close
  Upon the growing Boy,
    But He
Beholds the light, and whence it flows,
  He sees it in his joy;

The Youth, who daily farther from the east
  Must travel, still is Nature's Priest,
  And by the vision splendid
  Is on his way attended;
At length the Man perceives it die away,
And fade into the light of common day.

Earth fills her lap with pleasures of her own;
Yearnings she hath in her own natural kind,
And, even with something of a Mother's mind,
  And no unworthy aim,
  The homely Nurse doth all she can
To make her Foster-child, her Inmate Man,
  Forget the glories he hath known,
And that imperial palace whence he came.

Behold the Child among his new-born blisses,
A six years' Darling of a pigmy size!
See, where 'mid work of his own hand he lies,
Fretted by sallies of his mother's kisses,
With light upon him from his father's eyes!
See, at his feet, some little plan or chart,
Some fragment from his dream of human life,
Shaped by himself with newly-learned art;
  A wedding or a festival,
  A mourning or a funeral;
  And this hath now his heart,
  And unto this he frames his song:

Then will he fit his tongue
To dialogues of business, love, or strife;
But it will not be long,
Ere this be thrown aside,
And with new joy and pride
The little Actor cons another part;
Filling from time to time his 'humorous stage'
With all the Persons, down to palsied Age,
That Life brings with her in her equipage;
As if his whole vocation
Were endless imitation.

Thou, whose exterior semblance doth belie
Thy Soul's immensity;
Thou best Philosopher, who yet does keep
Thy heritage, thou Eye among the blind,
That, deaf and silent, read'st the eternal deep,
Haunted for ever by the eternal mind,—
Mighty Prophet! Seer blest!
On whom those truths do rest,
Which we are toiling all our lives to find,
In darkness lost, the darkness of the grave;
Thou, over whom thy Immortality
Broods like the Day, a Master o'er a Slave,
A Presence which is not to be put by;
Thou little Child, yet glorious in the might
Of heaven-born freedom on thy being's height,
Why with such earnest pains dost thou provoke

The years to bring the inevitable yoke,
Thus blindly with thy blessedness at strife?
Full soon thy Soul shall have her earthly freight,
And custom lie upon thee with a weight,
Heavy as frost, and deep almost as life!

O joy! that in our embers
Is something that doth live,
That nature yet remembers
What was so fugitive!
The thought of our past years in me doth breed
Perpetual benediction: not indeed
For that which is most worthy to be blest;
Delight and liberty, the simple creed
Of Childhood, whether busy or at rest,
With new-fledged hope still fluttering in his breast:—
Not for these I raise
The song of thanks and praise;
But for those obstinate questionings
Of sense and outward things,
Fallings from us, vanishings;
Blank misgivings of a Creature
Moving about in worlds not realised,
High instincts before which our mortal Nature
Did tremble like a guilty Thing surprised:
But for those first affections,
Those shadowy recollections,
Which, be they what they may,

Are yet the fountain light of all our day,
Are yet a master light of all our seeing;
    Uphold us, cherish, and have power to make
Our noisy years seem moments in the being
Of the eternal Silence: truths that wake,
        To perish never;
Which neither listlessness, nor mad endeavour,
        Nor Man nor Boy,
        Nor all that is at enmity with joy,
        Can utterly abolish or destroy!
        Hence in a season of calm weather
        Though inland far we be,
Our Souls have sight of that immortal sea
        Which brought us hither,
        Can in a moment travel thither,
And see the Children sport upon the shore,
And hear the mighty waters rolling evermore.

Then sing, ye Birds, sing, sing, a joyous song!
        And let the young Lambs bound
        As to the tabor's sound!
We in thought will join your throng,
        Ye that pipe and ye that play,
        Ye that through your hearts to-day
        Feel the gladness of the May!
What though the radiance which was once so bright
Be now for ever taken from my sight,
        Though nothing can bring back the hour

Of splendour in the grass, of glory in the flower;
        We will grieve not, rather find
        Strength in what remains behind;
        In the primal sympathy
        Which having been must ever be;
        In the soothing thoughts that spring
        Out of human suffering;
        In the faith that looks through death,
In years that bring the philosophic mind.

And O, ye Fountains, Meadows, Hills, and Groves,
Forebode not any severing of our loves!
Yet in my heart of hearts I feel your might;
I only have relinquished one delight
To live beneath your more habitual sway.
I love the Brooks which down their channels fret,
Even more than when I tripped lightly as they;
The innocent brightness of a new-born Day
        Is lovely yet;
The Clouds that gather round the setting sun
Do take a sober colouring from an eye
That hath kept watch o'er man's mortality;
Another race hath been, and other palms are won.
Thanks to the human heart by which we live,
Thanks to its tenderness, its joys, and fears,
To me the meanest flower that blows can give
Thoughts that do often lie too deep for tears.

William Wordsworth

Continuous as the stars that shine
And twinkle on the milky way,
They stretched in never-ending line
Along the margin of a bay . . ."

William Wordsworth:
" 'I wandered lonely as a cloud' "

Wild daffodils on the shore of Ullswater, near Gowbarrow
Park, where Dorothy and William saw them.

BROTHER AND SISTER IN HARMONY

Following their visit to Keswick the Wordsworths went to Eusemere to stay with the Clarksons, Dorothy remaining alone there for a week while William went to County Durham to see Mary Hutchinson. On April 15th brother and sister set out on foot, to make their return journey to Grasmere. Their road to Patterdale took them along the shore of Ullswater, through Watermillock and Gowbarrow Park. To quote a famous passage from Dorothy's *Journal,*

In the woods beyond Gowbarrow park we saw a few daffodils close to the water side. We fancied that the lake had floated the seeds ashore and that the little colony had so sprung up. But as we went along there were more and yet more and at last under the boughs of the trees, we saw that there was a long belt of them along the shore, about the breadth of a country turnpike road. I never saw daffodils so beautiful they grew among the mossy stones about and about them, some rested their heads upon these stones as on a pillow for weariness and the rest tossed and reeled and danced and seemed as if they verily laughed with the wind that blew upon them over the lake, they looked so gay ever glancing ever changing. This wind blew directly over the lake to them. There was here and there a little knot and a few stragglers a few yards higher up but they were so few as not to disturb the simplicity and unity and life of that one busy highway.

The Wordsworths spent the night at the little inn at Patterdale and next morning, Good Friday, resumed their journey home. When they reached Brothers Water, William sat down on the bridge, to write a descriptive poem, while Dorothy took a stroll. Again to quote another celebrated entry in her journal,

When I returned I found William writing a poem descriptive of the sights and sounds we saw and heard. There was the gentle flowing of the stream, the glittering lively lake, green fields without a living creature to be seen on them, behind us, a flat pasture with 42 cattle feeding to our left the road leading to the hamlet, no smoke there, the sun shone on the bare roofs. The people were at work ploughing, harrowing and sowing – lasses spreading dung, a dog's barking now and then, cocks crowing, birds twittering, the snow in patches at the top of the highest hills, yellow palms, purple and green twigs on the Birches, ashes with their glittering spikes quite

"Stone on Loughrigg Fell", one of William Green's "Studies from Nature" (1809). Green was encouraged by Thomas West to become an artist. In 1800, he settled in Ambleside and devoted the rest of his life to recording the Lake Country scenery and architecture. He opened Exhibition and Sale Rooms at Keswick and Ambleside from which he sold his enormous output of drawings to the Picturesque Tourists.

STONE ON LOUGHRIGG FELL.

bare. The hawthorn a bright green with black stems under the oak. The moss of the oak glossy. We then went on, passed two sisters at work, *they first passed us*, one with two pitch forks in her hand. The other had a spade. We had some talk with them. They laughed aloud after we were gone perhaps half in wantonness, half boldness. William finished his poem before we got to the foot of Kirkstone.

Spring strengthened into summer, the last that William and Dorothy would ever spend alone together. He continued to compose poem after poem, including some of his finest sonnets, and *The Leech Gatherer*. Brother and sister roamed and talked; sat in their little orchard; delighted in the birds and flowers. Mary had spoken of bringing her cat with her to Dove Cottage after her marriage, but Dorothy wrote firmly saying there could be no cat: "I spoke of the little Birds keeping us company."

Their evening walks continued to bring them more pleasure than walking at any other time of day. Their favourite place was White Moss Common where, in the gloaming, the white cotton-grass (the white moss of Cumbrian dialect) glimmered and

". . . a pool bare to the eye of heaven."

William Wordsworth: "The Leech Gatherer"

DEJECTION: AN ODE

Late, late yestreen I saw the new Moon,
With the old Moon in her arms;
And I fear, I fear, my Master dear!
We shall have a deadly storm.
Ballad of Sir Patrick Spence.

Well! If the Bard was weather-wise, who made
    The grand old ballad of Sir Patrick Spence,
    This night, so tranquil now, will not go hence
Unroused by winds, that ply a busier trade
Than those which mould yon cloud in lazy flakes,
Or the dull sobbing draft, that moans and rakes
        Upon the strings of this Eolian lute,
        Which better far were mute.
    For lo! the New-moon winter-bright!
    And overspread with phantom light,
    (With swimming phantom light o'erspread
    But rimmed and circled by a silver thread)
I see the old Moon in her lap, foretelling
    The coming on of rain and squally blast.
And oh! that even now the gust were swelling,
    And the slant night-shower driving loud and fast!
Those sounds which oft have raised me, whilst they awed,
    And sent my soul abroad,
Might now perhaps their wonted impulse give,
Might startle this dull pain, and make it move and live!

A grief without a pang, void, dark, and drear,
    A stifled, drowsy, unimpassioned grief,
    Which finds no natural outlet, no relief,
        In word, or sigh, or tear—
O Lady! in this wan and heartless mood,
To other thoughts by yonder throstle woo'd,
    All this long eve, so balmy and serene,
Have I been gazing on the western sky,
    And its peculiar tint of yellow green:
And still I gaze—and with how blank an eye!
And those thin clouds above, in flakes and bars,
That give away their motion to the stars;
Those stars, that glide behind them or between,
Now sparkling, now bedimmed, but always seen:
Yon crescent Moon as fixed as if it grew
In its own cloudless, starless lake of blue;
I see them all so excellently fair,
I see, not feel how beautiful they are!

    My genial spirits fail;
    And what can these avail
To lift the smothering weight from off my breast?
    It were a vain endeavour,
    Though I should gaze for ever

On that green light that lingers in the west:
I may not hope from outward forms to win
The passion and the life, whose fountains are within.

Oh Lady! we receive but what we give,
And in our life alone does nature live:
Ours is her wedding-garment, ours her shroud!
    And would we aught behold, of higher worth,
Than that inanimate cold world allowed
To the poor loveless ever-anxious crowd,
    Ah! from the soul itself must issue forth,
A light, a glory, a fair luminous cloud
        Enveloping the Earth—
And from the soul itself must there be sent
    A sweet and potent voice, of its own birth,
Of all sweet sounds the life and element!

O pure of heart! thou need'st not ask of me
What this strong music in the soul may be!
What, and wherein it doth exist,
This light, this glory, this fair luminous mist,
This beautiful and beauty-making power.
    Joy, virtuous Lady! Joy that ne'er was given,
Save to the pure, and in their purest hour,
Life, and Life's effluence, cloud at once and shower,
Joy, Lady! is the spirit and the power,
Which wedding Nature to us gives in dower,
    A new Earth and new Heaven,
Undreamt of by the sensual and the proud—
Joy is the sweet voice, Joy the luminous cloud—
        We in ourselves rejoice!
And thence flows all that charms or ear or sight,
    All melodies the echoes of that voice,
All colours a suffusion from that light.

There was a time when, though my path was rough,
    This joy within me dallied with distress,
And all misfortunes were but as the stuff
    Whence Fancy made me dreams of happiness:
For hope grew round me, like the twining vine,
And fruits, and foliage, not my own, seemed mine.
But now afflictions bow me down to earth:
Nor care I that they rob me of my mirth,
        But oh! each visitation
Suspends what nature gave me at my birth,
    My shaping spirit of Imagination.
For not to think of what I needs must feel,
    But to be still and patient, all I can;
And haply by abstruse research to steal
    From my own nature all the natural man—
    This was my sole resource, my only plan:
Till that which suits a part infects the whole,
And now is almost grown the habit of my soul.

Hence, viper thoughts, that coil around my mind,
    Reality's dark dream!
I turn from you, and listen to the wind,
    Which long has raved unnoticed. What a scream
Of agony by torture lengthened out
That lute sent forth! Thou Wind, that ravest without,
    Bare craig, or mountain-tairn, or blasted tree,
Or pine-grove whither woodman never clomb,
Or lonely house, long held the witches' home,
Methinks were fitter instruments for thee,
Mad Lutanist! who in this month of showers,
Of dark brown gardens, and of peeping flowers,
Mak'st Devils' yule, with worse than wintry song,
The blossoms, buds, and timorous leaves among.
    Thou Actor, perfect in all tragic sounds!
Though mighty Poet, e'en to frenzy bold!
    What tell'st thou now about?
    'Tis of the rushing of a host in rout,
    With groans of trampled men, with smarting wounds—
At once they groan with pain, and shudder with the cold!
But hush! there is a pause of deepest silence!
    And all that noise, as of a rushing crowd,
With groans, and tremulous shudderings—all is over—
    It tells another tale, with sounds less deep and loud!
    A tale of less affright,
    And tempered with delight,
    As Otway's self had framed the tender lay,
    'Tis of a little child
    Upon a lonesome wild,
Not far from home, but she hath lost her way:
And now moans low in bitter grief and fear,
And now screams loud, and hopes to make her mother hear.

'Tis midnight, but small thoughts have I of sleep:
Full seldom may my friend such vigils keep!
Visit her, gentle Sleep! with wings of healing,
    And may this storm be but a mountain-birth,
May all the stars hang bright above her dwelling,
    Silent as though they watched the sleeping Earth!
    With light heart may she rise,
    Gay fancy, cheerful eyes,
    Joy lift her spirit, joy attune her voice;
To her may all things live, from pole to pole,
Their life the eddying of her living soul!
    O simple spirit, guided from above,
Dear Lady! friend devoutest of my choice,
Thus mayest thou ever, evermore rejoice.

                                    Samuel Taylor Coleridge

shone with silver magic. Dorothy's *Journal* entry for June 1st captures for us the enchantment of the place: "It was a lovely night. The clouds of the western sky reflected a saffron light upon the upper end of the lake. All was still . . . There was an alpine fire-like red upon the tops of the mountains . . . This White Moss a place made for all kinds of beautiful works of art and nature, woods and valleys, fairy valleys and fairy Tairns, miniature mountains, alps above alps."

Feeling between the pair became, at times, too deep for words. "After we came in we sate in silence at the window – I on a chair and William with his head on my shoulder. We were deep in Silence and Love, a blessed hour."

It was not an easy period of their lives. Dorothy's *Journal* for these last months alone together make constant mention of her "uneasy spirits" and sick headaches and of William's insomnia. To soothe him Dorothy, at his request, would repeat to him over and over again, *This is the spot*, one of William's favourite poems writen by him for, and about, Dorothy. She also read him Milton's sonnets, which moved him increasingly towards composing sonnets himself; sonnets which Coleridge was later to describe as being written, "in the spirit of the best of Milton".

THIS IS THE SPOT

This is the spot:—how mildly does the sun
Shine in between the fading leaves! the air
In the habitual silence of this wood
Is more than silent; and this bed of heath—
Where shall we find so sweet a resting-place?
Come, let me see thee sink into a dream
Of quiet thoughts, protracted till thine eye
Be calm as water when the winds are gone
And no one can tell whither. My sweet Friend,
We two have had such happy hours together
That my heart melts in me to think of it.

William Wordsworth

The "white moss", as Cotton Grass is known in Cumbria, on White Moss Common where William and Dorothy loved to stroll.

I WANDERED LONELY AS A CLOUD

I wandered lonely as a cloud
That floats on high o'er vales and hills,
When all at once I saw a crowd,
A host, of golden daffodils;
Beside the lake, beneath the trees,
Fluttering and dancing in the breeze.

Continuous as the stars that shine
And twinkle on the milky way,
They stretched in never-ending line
Along the margin of a bay:
Ten thousand saw I at a glance,
Tossing their heads in sprightly dance.

The waves beside them danced; but they
Out-did the sparkling waves in glee:
A poet could not but be gay,
In such a jocund company:
I gazed—and gazed—but little thought
What wealth the show to me had brought:

For oft, when on my couch I lie
In vacant or in pensive mood,
They flash upon that inward eye
Which is the bliss of solitude:
And then my heart with pleasure fills,
And dances with the daffodils.

William Wordsworth

TO SLEEP

A flock of sheep that leisurely pass by,
One after one; the sound of rain, and bees
Murmuring; the fall of rivers, winds and seas,
Smooth fields, white sheets of water, and
                           pure sky;
I have thought of all by turns, and yet do lie
Sleepless! and soon the small birds' melodies
Must hear, first uttered from my orchard trees;
And the first cuckoo's melancholy cry.
Even thus last night, and two nights more, I lay
And could not win thee, Sleep! by any stealth:
So do not let me wear to-night away:
Without Thee what is all the morning's wealth?
Come, blessed barrier between day and day,
Dear mother of fresh thoughts and joyous health!

William Wordsworth

Brother and sister left Grasmere on July 9th and travelled down to London, which they left early on the morning of July 31st. Dorothy's *Journal* reads, "We mounted the Dover Coach at Charing Cross. It was a beautiful morning. The City, St Paul's, with the River and a multitude of little Boats, made a most beautiful sight as we crossed Westminster Bridge.

The houses were not overhung by their cloud of smoke and they were spread out endlessly, yet the sun shone so brightly with such a pure light that there was even something like the purity of one of nature's own grand spectacles."

An auspicious start to their three weeks visit in France, staying in Calais with Annette and little

"I . . . yet do lie
Sleepless! and soon the small birds' melodies
Must hear . . .
And the first cuckoo's melancholy cry."

The summer nights of silvery gloaming slip into silvery dawn almost without any intervening darkness; sleep is the only 'barrier between day and day".

COMPOSED UPON WESTMINSTER BRIDGE
SEPTEMBER 3, 1802

Earth has not anything to show more fair:
Dull would he be of soul who could pass by
A sight so touching in its majesty:
This City now doth, like a garment, wear
The beauty of the morning; silent, bare,
Ships, towers, domes, theatres, and temples lie
Open unto the fields, and to the sky;
All bright and glittering in the smokeless air.
Never did sun more beautifully steep
In his first splendour, valley, rock, or hill;
Ne'er saw I, never felt, a calm so deep!
The river glideth at his own sweet will:
Dear God! the very houses seem asleep;
And all that mighty heart is lying still!

William Wordsworth

LONDON, 1802

Milton! thou shouldst be living at this hour:
England hath need of thee: she is a fen
Of stagnant waters: altar, sword, and pen,
Fireside, the heroic wealth of hall and bower,
Have forfeited their ancient English dower
Of inward happiness. We are selfish men;
Oh! raise us up, return to us again;
And give us manners, virtue, freedom, power.
Thy soul was like a Star, and dwelt apart;
Thou hadst a voice whose sound was like the sea:
Pure as the naked heavens, majestic, free,
So didst thou travel on life's common way,
In cheerful godliness; and yet thy heart
The lowliest duties on herself did lay.

William Wordsworth

'THE COCK IS CROWING'

The cock is crowing,
The stream is flowing,
The small birds twitter,
The lake doth glitter,
The green field sleeps in the sun;
The oldest and youngest
Are at work with the strongest;
The cattle are grazing,
Their heads never raising;
There are forty feeding like one!

Like an army defeated
The snow hath retreated,
And now doth fare ill
On the top of the bare hill;
The Ploughboy is whooping—anon—anon:
There's joy in the mountains;
There's life in the fountains;
Small clouds are sailing,
Blue sky prevailing;
The rain is over and gone!

William Wordsworth

Caroline – three weeks which passed most agreeably, with much sea bathing and strolling on the cliffs. For Wordsworth, France was now a very different place from what it had been ten years before when, himself glowing with ardour for liberty, equality and fraternity, and in love with Annette, he had found it "a country in romance." Now Napoleon was transforming it into a juggernaut; for years to come his *Grande Armée* would cast its shadow, and peace, liberty and brother-

WASDALE HEAD lies tucked in the very heart of the mountains, as we see it here, with Great Gable (in former times Great Gavel) in the centre, presenting its gable, or gavel end; Kirk Fell to the left, and Lingmell (an outlying spur of Scafell Pike) on the right. Village was, and is, too grandiose a name for this cluster of small toftsteads (shown here in 1781) rejoicing in the most precise topography: Row Head, Middle Row, and Row Foot. Wasdale Head is a chapelry in the parish of Eskdale and the resident population of the place is said never to have exceeded fifty persons. The documented history of Wasdale Head reaches back to the twelfth century, with Burnthwaite (the group of buildings in the background) as one of the largest and earliest of all the sheep farms in the region. Note the walled fields in the dale bottom and clambering up the fellside. Coleridge's host in August 1802 (as when the first came with Wordsworth in 1799) was Thomas Tyson of Row Head.

hood would be nothing but a forlorn dream. Nor, Wordsworth felt, did England, stagnant and weary, hold out much hope for the future. He stood on the French shore, gazing across the Straits of Dover:

> . . . with many a fear
> For my dear Country, many heartfelt sighs . . .
>
> *"Fair Star of Evening"*

HAPPINESS AGAINST THE ODDS

For the Coleridges at Greta Hall, life had become much happier, following a reconciliation and a determined attempt by both parties "to live in peace and love", although this did not mean that Coleridge could give up opium; so the root cause of all his troubles was still with him. Nonetheless the greatly improved domestic atmosphere helped him to recover his ability to work. His physical condition showed improvement likewise and on August 1st he set out on a solo pedestrian tour, the highlight of which was to be an ascent of the Scafells; "Believed by the Shepherds here to be higher than either Helvellyn or Skiddaw" (as he wrote to a friend) and virgin territory so far as all but the shepherds themselves were concerned.

On August 1st Coleridge set out from Keswick over Newland Hause to Buttermere, from thence by Floutern to Ennerdale, from Ennerdale via Egremont to Wastdale Foot and from there up to Wasdale Head. He arrived in Nether Wasdale in the early afternoon of August 4th and, after taking refreshment at the inn, he trudged on up the valley, past Wastwater and the Screes, to Wasdale Head. In a letter to Sarah Hutchinson he described the Screes, that vast cascade of stones that pours down the north-western face of Illgill Head and Whin Rigg: "[a] huge facing of rock . . . with deep perpendiular Ravines, from the Top two thirds down / other Ravines slanting athwart down them/the whole wrinkled & torrent-worn and barely patched with Moss – and all this reflected, turned in Pillars & a whole new-world of Images, in the water."

Coleridge slept the night at Wasdale Head and next morning set off to climb Scafell, taking the pony track up on to Burn Moor and from there toiling up Green How until he gained Black Crag and the

summit of Scafell. Here he stood revelling in a view which extended from the Pennines to the Irish Sea. Then he moved forward until he stood on the top of Scafell Crag, with Deep Gill beneath him, and the giant rock masses of Pinnacle and Pisgah (names not yet invented in his day) immediately before him: a landscape of "enormous & more than perpendicular Precipices." He became immensely excited. "O! what a look down just under my Feet! The frightfullest Cove that might ever be seen . . . I have no shadow of hesitation in saying that the Coves & Precipices of Helvellyn are nothing to these!"

A threatening thunderstorm at last forced him to search for a way down to Upper Eskdale (his goal was Tawes House near Brotherilkeld). He quickly came face to face with an obstacle: "I . . . found myself cut

THE SAME VIEW as that which sent Coleridge into raptures in 1802: looking from the summit of Scafell, "A great mountain of stones," towards Great Gable; a landscape, as he put it, of "Precipices and Bull's Brows," and adding, "I have no shadow of hesitation in saying that the Coves & Precipices of Helvellyn are nothing to these!" He concluded, "Of all earthly things which I have beheld, the view of Scafell and from Scafell . . . is the most heart-exciting."

smooth, perpendicular precipices. Soon he began to suspect that he ought not to go on, "but then unfortunately tho' I could with ease drop down a smooth rock 7 feet high, I could not *climb* it / so go on I must / and on I went / . . . and now I had only two more to drop down / to return was impossible – but of those two the first was tremendous / it was twice my own height, & the ledge at the Bottom was exceedingly narrow, that if I dropt down upon it I must of necessity have fallen backwards & of course killed myself." Peering down at the ledge he noticed on it a pile of stones and guessed that they had been placed there by a shepherd, attempting to climb up to a crag-fast sheep that Coleridge had seen, dead, at the bottom of the third precipice he had dropped down. "As I was looking at these I glanced my eye to the left, & observed that the Rock was rent from top to bottom – I measured the Breadth of the Rent, and found there was no danger of my being *wedged* in / so I put my Knap-sack round to my side, & slipped down as between two walls, without any danger or difficulty – the next Drop brought me down on to the Ridge . . ."

This descent of Coleridge from off Scafell Crag is the first recorded climb in rock-climbing history. Rock-fall has since changed the appearance of Broad Stand and Scafell Chimney (the part of the rock face where he had his adventure) but it is nowadays generally accepted that it was down Scafell Chimney, and not Broad Stand, that Coleridge made his pioneer route. It was certainly bona fide rock-climbing, upon serious rock; and that Coleridge survived is proof of his remarkable athleticism and self control in situations of physical danger. In short it is obvious that Coleridge was a natural mountaineer of no mean order and had he lived a few decades later in time he might well have been one of that select band of Cambridge men who pioneered so many climbs.

"O how I wished," he mused, when he had safely made his way down Cam Spout Gully and Upper Eskdale in a tumult of thunder and echoes, "that I might wander about for a Month together, in the

off from a most sublime Crag-summit [Scafell Pike] that seemed to rival Sca'Fell Man in height, & to outdo it in fierceness. A ridge of Hill [Mickledore] lay low & divided this crag [Scafell Pike] & Broad-crag [old shepherds' name for Scafell Crag] even as the Hyphen divides the words broad & crag. I determined to go thither."

So down he went, dropping a series of small,

THE EXCURSION
(excerpt)

Many are the notes
Which, in his tuneful course, the wind draws
forth
From rocks, woods, caverns, heaths, and dashing
shores;
And well those lofty brethren bear their part
In the wild concert–chiefly when the storm
Rides high; then all the upper air they fill
With roaring sound, that ceases not to flow,
Like smoke, along the level of the blast,
In mighty current; theirs, too, is the song
Of stream and headlong flood that seldom fails;
And, in the grim and breathless hour of noon,
Methinks that I have heard them echo back
The thunder's greeting. Nor have nature's laws
Left them ungifted with a power to yield
Music of finer tone; a harmony,
So do I call it, though it be the hand
Of silence, though there be no voice;–the clouds,
The mist, the shadows, light of golden suns,
Motions of moonlight, all come thither–touch,
And have an answer–thither come, and shape
A language not unwelcome to sick hearts
And idle spirits . . .

William Wordsworth

HERDWICK SHEEP crossing the ancient wool-pack bridge in Upper Eskdale; they are making their way up the dalehead towards Throstlegarth (Coleridge, coming down to Tawes House from Scafell, crossed this bridge in the opposite direction). The Cistercian monks had an important "saetr", or summer shieling, in Throstlegarth, an area of green alps lying above Upper Eskdale waterfalls; which doubtless explains the presence of this wool-pack bridge, as the sheep would have been clipped in the folds of Throstlegarth and the wool brought down by pack-ponies.

stormiest month of the year, among these Places, so lonely & savage & full of sounds!" An echo of Wordsworth's "Solitary" in *The Excursion*:

Following Coleridge's return to Greta Hall Charles and Mary Lamb came to stay. Lamb, whose friendship with Coleridge dated back to schooldays at Christ's Hospital had already been invited to the Lakes twice, but on each occasion had refused the invitation. A dedicated Cockney, he had firmly

declared, "Hills, woods, lakes and mountains, to the eternal devil . . . I am not romance-bit about Nature."

However, at last he had accepted. Coleridge showed him "all the wonders of the country," as Lamb afterwards wrote to a friend. Keswick, Grasmere, Ambleside, Ullswater; over Helvellyn; up Skiddaw; "And I have waded up the bed of Lodore. In fine," concluded Lamb, "I have satisfied myself that there is such a thing as that which tourists call *romantic,*

CAM SPOUT CRAG (enclosing the Gully), Dow Crag and Little Narrowcove, the ragged ramparts of the Scafell Pikes, are seen on the left of this picture. Note the huge boulders in the left middle distance: Coleridge, when he first saw them, supposed these to be small cottages, or cabins. This lonely place, miles from any road and in Coleridge's day known only to shepherds, is even now only accessible to hardy walkers and climbers.

DEVOKE WATER lies west of the old road across Birker Fell, linking Eskdale with Dunnerdale. Coleridge's notebook entries suggest a mood of anti-climax once he had left Eskdale and the Scafells behind him on his pedestrian tour; lovely as Devoke Water is, it could not compare with his experiences of the past few days. He was searching for Barnscar, legendary ancient city, but like many a disappointed traveller since, was unable to find any trace. "However, the view is very fine. Sauce better than the fish . . ."

which I very much suspected before; they make such a spluttering about it."

The weather was wet during most of Lamb's visit and Lodore, as a result, was (Coleridge wrote in a high Romantic passage intended for subsequent publication), "Finer than I ever saw it before . . . Lodore is the precipitation of the fallen Angels from Heaven, Flight & Confusion, & Distraction, but all harmonized into one majestic Thing."

NEW DOMESTIC BLISS

The Wordsworths arrived at Gallow Hill, Mary Hutchinson's farmstead home, on September 24th; Mary looked "fat and well", Dorothy noted. For most of the stay at Gallow Hill Dorothy, however, was ill. She continues, "On Monday 4th October 1802, my Brother William was married to Mary Hutchinson . . .

At a little after 8 o'clock I saw them go down the avenue towards the Church. William had parted from me upstairs. I gave him the wedding ring – with how deep a blessing! I took it from my forefinger where I had worn it the whole of the night before – he slipped it again on to my finger and blessed me fervently. When they were absent . . . I kept myself as quiet as I could, till Sara [Hutchinson] came upstairs to me and said, "They are coming." This forced me

from the bed where I lay and I moved I knew not how straight forward, faster than my strength could carry me till I met my beloved William and fell upon his bosom."

ON THEIR HIGHLAND TOUR of 1803 the trio, William, Dorothy and Coleridge, accustomed to the greener Lake Country, travelled through scenery totally wanting, in "cultivated Land & happy Cottages." However they were enchanted by the heather, "The pale-purple, the deep crimson, or rose-coloured Purple" which gave, as Coleridge remarked in his notebook, "A sort of feeling of Shot silk and ribbon finery."

Immediately the wedding breakfast was over the extraordinary trio, William, Mary, and Dorothy, set out on the two day journey to Dove Cottage, where they arrived on the evening of October 6th. Molly Fisher, overjoyed, was waiting to greet them. Dorothy and William had been absent for three long months. "We went by candle light into the garden, and we were astonished by the growth of Brooms, Portugal Laurels, etc."

Dorothy attempted to take up her old way of life as though virtually nothing had been changed by William's marriage, but her *Journal* faltered and finally petered out, a sure sign in itself of fundamental

change. Mary, who had kept house for a farmer brother, was used to being a busy housekeeper and Dorothy found herself increasingly involved in busy, bustling domestic activity. With the birth of Mary's first child on June 18th 1803, more and more of the household management fell upon Dorothy. Similarly, less and less of Coleridge was seen at Dove Cottage: the birth of his third child, a daughter, Sara, at Christmas, 1802, some touring in Wales with Tom Wedgwood, and ill health brought about by walking over Kirkstone Pass in a violent storm, combined to keep him away from the Wordsworths. A Highland Tour, made with Dorothy and William in August of

that year was not a success. The trio parted company at Arrochar and Coleridge made a remarkably active solo pedestrian tour: Glen Coe, Loch Ness, Aviemore, Kingussie, Loch Tummel, Kenmore, Perth – two hundred and sixty three miles in eight days.

ADDICTION INTENSIFIES

But opium, and the Cumbrian damp, were totally undermining his health and it was decided that he *must* try a warmer climate. In early 1804 he set sail for Malta, leaving his wife and children under the care of Robert Southey, who together with Edith, and another Fricker sister, Mary Lovell, had taken up residence at Greta Hall. Coleridge spoke vaguely of being absent for twelve months, but as it turned out he did not return to England until May 1806 and did not arrive back at Greta Hall until the end of October. He was shattered with opium, bloated, dazed, and without

THE EXILE: Coleridge in Rome, 1805, where he wintered, en route for England, after sixteen months in Malta, during which he had privately wrestled (unsuccessfully) with opium, and had served with distinction as temporary Public Secretary, a post only second in civil dignity to that of the Governor, Sir Alexander Ball. The artist, Washington Allston, was the first important American Romantic painter; he studied art in London, Paris and Rome, where he first met Coleridge, the two men forming a close and lasting friendship.

preamble told his wife (who, with the children, had greeted him joyously, "Papa is home!") that he could no longer live with her: life with her was unendurable for him and there must be a separation (divorce, in those days, was unobtainable). It was Coleridge's intention to live with the Wordsworths, taking his two sons with him.

Before many weeks had passed Coleridge was writing from Coleorton (where he and the Wordsworths were to pass the winter) blandly remarking that as the Southeys would be leaving Greta Hall soon, Coleridge and the Wordsworths would be setting up house there together. Although there had been some talk of the Southeys leaving Greta Hall for the south there had been no suggestion that Mrs Coleridge should accompany them. All her plans were built around her remaining at Greta Hall. If her estranged husband moved into the vacant "front house" with the Wordsworths she would be obliged to quit,

Hartley Colerdige in his eleventh year; a steel engraving by William Holl, from an oil sketch by Wilkie, owned by Sir George Beaumont. This portrait was painted during the period that the little boy was taken away from Greta Hall by his father to pass the winter at Coleorton and the spring in London.

turned out of her own home and with nowhere to go. Southey, learning abruptly that he was expected to vacate Greta Hall to humour Coleridge and his whim to live with the Wordsworths, responded with a vehement, "That be hanged for a tale!" A letter was at once penned to Coleridge: Southey had no intention of leaving Greta Hall, it was out of the question, and as for Mrs Coleridge and the children, they would remain there with the Southeys. In this abrupt, wholly unpremeditated fashion Southey, who had gone to Keswick on the understanding it would be for eighteen months or so at the longest, found himself settled there for good. And, what was more, landed with his sister-in-law and her three children.

GRETA HALL'S NEW MASTER

This was not to say that Southey did not like the Lakes, and was not happy there. During Coleridge's absence in Malta Southey had settled down very pleasantly as master of Greta Hall, and became increasingly the literary lion of the Lakes. Although he has now largely been forgotten, in his own day he was, as Poet Laureate, author and reviewer, one of the most famous men on the contemporary literary scene, far eclipsing Wordsworth, and for much of the time outshining Coleridge. It was not until 1813 that Southey became Laureate, but his name as a man of letters was becoming established by the time he arrived in Keswick in 1803 and he quickly dropped into the pattern of life that he was to follow for the next forty years: the winter devoted to reviewing, writing books and composing reams of verse, and the summer to being lionized by a non-stop flow of Lakers; many of them famous, or at least fashionable people. For in the first half of the nineteenth century Keswick was one of *the* most desirable resorts in "the civilized world, for the discerning and the select", as Mrs Coleridge rather smugly wrote to one of her lady acquaintances.

The letters of Southey and of Mrs Coleridge give us succinct glimpses of the many visitors who, in the height of the season, arrived on the doorstep of Greta Hall, either by invitation (Southey was a most generous and affable host) or bearing notes of introduction. Aspiring poets in swarms turned up from out of the blue, anxious to show their own poems to Southey: "Usually very *bad* poems, in at least two volumes," he groaned.

Southey's own reputation as a poet had been made while he was still only in his early twenties. His *Joan of Arc*, an epic poem, published in 1795, had

ROBERT SOUTHEY in the study at Greta Hall, in 1804. This was formerly Coleridge's study but he was now in Malta and Southey was quietly settling into his new role as budding Literary Lion of the Lakes and (as Coleridge put it) "Vice-fathership" of the Coleridge children.

received encouraging reviews and had opened to him the doors of literary employment. His shorter, lighter verses met with popular approval; he composed swiftly and easily, with a deft touch. But his ambition was to win fame with his epic poems. *Madoc*, which he hoped to leave "to posterity" as he optimistically wrote when he started work on it in 1795, was finished in 1799, then he laid aside until he

Mrs. SARA COLERIDGE, aged thirty-nine: a miniature portrait painted by Matilda Betham in 1809, when she spent the summer and autumn as a guest at Greta Hall and did miniatures of the entire family. Southey tells us of an amusing incident during a ladies' excursion up Skiddaw. On the way down, Mrs. Coleridge (famous for scrapes and ridiculous disasters, often in the course of Picturesque excursions with visiting Lakers seeking sublime experiences) "got into a bog some way above her knees, and I saved her life! . . . Afterwards I washed her petticoat in one of the gills, and carried it home on my stick."

went to Keswick, when he extensively rewrote it. Based on the story of Madoc, the son of a twelfth century king of Wales, it was received with moderate enthusiasm, despite the fact that Southey introduced the Aztecs, whom he thought were bound to have

popular appeal. *Thalaba the Destroyer*, described by Southey as an "Arabesque ornament of an Arabian tale" was packed with wizards, sorceresses, a female vampire, magic stones, charms, enchanted ostrich eggs, revels and massacres. Published in 1801 it was scathingly reviewed by Francis Jeffrey, editor of the newly founded *Edinburgh Review*. Jeffrey complained that the poem had no originality and was "made up of scraps of old sermons." He went on to take an overall swipe at what he called "this new school of Lake poets", lumping Southey, Wordsworth and Coleridge together as a "mischievous fraternity" living on the "squashy banks of a lake", and "debasing those feelings which poetry is designed to communicate."

Sir Walter Scott was a great admirer of Southey's poetry, indeed it was Scott who put Southey's name forward as Laureate. Wordsworth, during his 1803 Scottish tour, had met Scott and two years later Scott visited the Lakes. Together with Humphry Davy and Wordsworth, he climbed Helvellyn, afterwards going on to visit at Greta Hall. Helvellyn held especial Romantic interest that season, owing to the recent tragedy of a young man named Charles Gough, who had slipped from the summit crags and fallen to his death. His dog had remained guarding his body for three months, being at last spied by a shepherd, who had then discovered the corpse. Scott, like Wordsworth, was deeply moved by this episode; each man composed a poem on the subject.

AIRA FORCE, a foremost Picturesque attraction, is a waterfall lying on the fringe of Gowbarrow Park, beside Ullswater. In 1807, Wordworth, pressed by Dorothy and Mary to earn money to provide furnishings for their new home Allan Bank, tried his hand at popular ballad-style poems, one of them being "The Somnambulist". The ballad told a tale of blighted love; that of the palpitating Emma and her knight Sir Eglamore. He departed for the wars leaving Emma to droop and take to sleep-walking. One evening, while the melancholy somnambulist was roaming by Aira Force, he unexpectedly returned. He tried to seize his beloved in his arms, whereat she started awake, screamed, and fell backwards into the waterfall's basin, where she drowned. Overwhelmed with grief, Sir Eglamore built himself a cell in the glen and spent the remainder of his days as an anchorite. Allom, in this illustration, simultaneously depicted a pair of lovers, the cell and the ghostly form of Sir Eglamore perched high on the waterfall, forever surveying the scene of the tragedy!

HELVELLYN

I climb'd the dark brow of the mighty Helvellyn,
    Lakes and mountains beneath me gleam'd misty
                       and wide;
All was still, save by fits, when the eagle was yelling,
    And starting around me the echoes replied.
On the right, Striden-edge round the Red-tarn was bending,
And Catchedicam its left verge was defending,
One huge nameless rock in the front was ascending,
    When I mark'd the sad spot where the wanderer
                     had died.

Dark green was that spot 'mid the brown mountain-heather,
    Where the Pilgrim of Nature lay stretch'd in decay
Like the corpse of an outcast abandon'd to weather,
    Till the mountain winds wasted the tenantless clay.
Not yet quite deserted, though lonely extended,
For, faithful in death, his mute favourite tended,
The much-loved remains of her master defended,
    And chased the hill-fox and the raven away.

How long didst thou think that his silence was slumber?
    When the wind waved his garment, how oft didst
                     thou start?
How many long days and long weeks didst thou number,
    Ere he faded before thee, the friend of thy heart?
And oh! was it meet, that—no requiem read o'er him—
No mother to weep, and no friend to deplore him,
And thou, little guardian, alone stretch'd before him—
    Unhonour'd the Pilgrim from life should depart?

When a Prince to the fate of the Peasant has yielded,
    The tapestry waves dark round the dim-lighted hall;
With scutcheons of silver the coffin is shielded,
    And pages stand mute by the canopied pall:
Through courts, at deep midnight, the torches are gleaming;
In the proudly-arch'd chapel the banners are beaming,
Far adown the long aisle sacred music is streaming,
    Lamenting a Chief of the people should fall.

But meeter for thee, gentle lover of nature,
    To lay down thy head like the meek mountain lamb,
When, wilder'd, he drops from some cliff huge in stature,
    And draws his last sob by the side of his dam.
And more stately thy couch by this desert lake lying,
Thy obsequies sung by the grey plover flying,
With one faithful friend but to witness thy dying,
    In the arms of Helvellyn and Catchedicam.

                             Sir Walter Scott

FIDELITY

A barking sound the Shepherd hears,
A cry as of a dog or fox;
He halts—and searches with his eyes
Among the scattered rocks:
And now at distance can discern
A stirring in a brake of fern;
And instantly a dog is seen,
Glancing through that covert green.

The Dog is not of mountain breed;
Its motions, too, are wild and shy;
With something, as the Shepherd thinks,
Unusual in its cry:
Nor is there any one in sight
All round, in hollow or on height;
Nor shout, nor whistle strikes his ear;
What is the creature doing here?

It was a cove, a huge recess,
That keeps, till June, December's snow;
A lofty precipice in front,
A silent tarn below!
Far in the bosom of Helvellyn,
Remote from public road or dwelling,
Pathway, or cultivated land;
From trace of human foot or hand.

There sometimes doth a leaping fish
Send through the tarn a lonely cheer;
The crags repeat the raven's croak,
In symphony austere;
Thither the rainbow comes—the cloud—
And mists that spread the flying shroud;
And sunbeams; and the sounding blast,
That, if it could, would hurry past;
But that enormous barrier holds it fast.

Not free from boding thoughts, a while
The Shepherd stood; then makes his way
O'er rocks and stones, following the Dog
As quickly as he may;
Nor far had gone before he found
A human skeleton on the ground;
The appalled Discoverer with a sigh
Looks round, to learn the history.

From those abrupt and perilous rocks
The Man had fallen, that place of fear!
At length upon the Shepherd's mind
It breaks, and all is clear:
He instantly recalled the name,
And who he was, and whence he came;
Remembered, too, the very day
On which the Traveller passed this way.

But hear a wonder, for whose sake
This lamentable tale I tell!
A lasting monument of words
This wonder merits well.
The Dog, which still was hovering nigh,
Repeating the same timid cry,
This Dog, had been through three months' space
A dweller in that savage place.

Yes, proof was plain that, since the day
When this ill-fated Traveller died,
The Dog had watched about the spot,
Or by his master's side:
How nourished here through such long time
He knows, who gave that love sublime;
And gave that strength of feeling, great
Above all human estimate!

William Wordsworth

THE EAST INDIAMAN, "Earl of Abergavenney", with 387 persons aboard, was wrecked off Portland Bill on February 5th, 1805, and her captain John Wordsworth, was drowned together with 232 passengers and crew members. The casualty list was so high because, although in sight of shore, the passengers, terrified by the high seas, refused to entrust themselves to the ship's boats. At last a sloop put out and took survivors from the rigging of the sinking ship, twenty at a time; others managed to drift to safety on bits of wreckage. Two enquiries into the loss of the vessel were held by the Court of the East India Company: it was unanimously agreed that the calamity was not the fault of the ship's commander or members of her company.

TRAGEDY FOR THE WORDSWORTHS

The year of 1805 was crucial for William Wordsworth. On February 5th John Wordsworth was drowned when his ship was wrecked, a tragedy which had a profound and lasting effect upon William. "A deep distress hath humanised my Soul . . ." he was to write in his *Elegiac Stanzas* in commemoration of his brother:

> Farewell, farewell the heart that lives alone,
> Housed in a dream . . .

Certainly the Wordsworths displayed immense humanity in the matter of having Coleridge come to live with them, first at Coleorton, then at Allan Bank, a large new villa overlooking Grasmere, into which they moved in 1809 as a result of their growing family (two sons and two daughters), not to mention Coleridge. Coleorton had already taught them the impossibility of Coleridge as a member of a household. They could not make him happy, nor could they wean him from opium as they had hoped would be the case. The changes in his character which the drug had brought about had made him a most disruptive personality, but the Wordsworths, having promised that he, once separated from his wife, might have a home with them, stood by their word, even though they realized that this could only bring them trouble.

ELEGIAC STANZAS

Suggested by a picture of Peele Castle, in A Storm, painted by
Sir George Beaumont

I was thy neighbour once, thou rugged Pile!
Four summer weeks I dwelt in sight of thee:
I saw thee every day; and all the while
Thy Form was sleeping on a glassy sea.

So pure the sky, so quiet was the air!
So like, so very like, was day to day!
Whene'er I looked, thy Image still was there;
It trembled, but it never passed away.

How perfect was the calm! it seemed no sleep;
No mood, which season takes away, or brings:
I could have fancied that the mighty Deep
Was even the gentlest of all gentle Things.

Ah! then, if mine had been the Painter's hand,
To express what then I saw; and add the gleam,
The light that never was, on sea or land,
The consecration, and the Poet's dream;

I would have planted thee, thou hoary Pile
Amid a world how different from this!
Beside a sea that could not cease to smile;
On tranquil land, beneath a sky of bliss. . .

A Picture had it been of lasting ease,
Elysian quiet, without toil or strife;
No motion but the moving tide, a breeze,
Or merely silent Nature's breathing life.

Such, in the fond illusion of my heart,
Such Picture would I at that time have made:
And seen the soul of truth in every part,
A steadfast peace that might not be betrayed.

So once it would have been,—'tis so no more;
I have submitted to a new control:
A power is gone, which nothing can restore;
A deep distress hath humanised my Soul.

Then, Beaumont, Friend! who would have been the Friend,
If he had lived, of Him whom I deplore,
This work of thine I blame not, but commend;
This sea in anger, and that dismal shore.

O 'tis a passionate Work!—yet wise and well,
Well chosen is the spirit that is here;
That Hulk which labours in the deadly swell,
This rueful sky, this pageantry of fear!

And this huge Castle, standing here sublime,
I love to see the look with which it braves,
Cased in the unfeeling armour of old time,
The lightning, the fierce wind, and trampling waves.

Farewell, farewell the heart that lives alone,
Housed in a dream, at distance from the Kind!
Such happiness, wherever it be known,
Is to be pitied; for 'tis surely blind . . .

William Wordsworth

148

THE FRIENDSHIP FALTERS

In point of fact Coleridge, having once "separated" from Sara, spent increasing periods of time with her at Greta Hall, a somewhat typical course of behaviour. In 1810 he and Wordsworth had their famous quarrel. This was due to a culmination of many things, but chiefly arose because Wordsworth warned a mutual friend not to offer Coleridge accommodation in London because of his opium addiction which made him a "positive nuisance" in any and every household of which he became a part. The quarrel was not patched up for almost three years, by which time Coleridge had deserted the Lakes for ever. And not only the Lakes but, it seemed, his wife and children too. Southey resignedly shouldered the responsibility of providing them with a surrogate father and keeping a roof over their heads.

LIFE AT GRETA HALL

It was Southey's belief that no household was complete without a kitten rising six weeks and a child rising three years. Under his regime Greta Hall was kept well supplied with both kittens and children.

Southey and Edith had seven children in all, and with Mrs Coleridge's three, and Mary Lovell's one, not to mention small visiting Wordsworths and the neighbouring Calvert offspring, Greta Hall was to resound to nursery romps and games for many years to come. As for cats, Greta Hall abounded with tribes of them.

All the children had nicknames: little Edith May was "Shedaw"; Herbert, because of his round face as a baby, was the Moon, or "Juvenile Moon" as distinct from Mrs Coleridge who, as roundfaced now in her middle years as Herbert was in his infancy, was the "Venerable Moon", or simply "The Venerable." Kate, solemn faced and wide-eyed, was "Countess Pussykate." Isabel was simply "Belle." Little Sara Coleridge, because of her small stature, was "Shortykins", or "The Short". Derwent Coleridge, since his broad

Although no sketches or paintings survive depicting social and domestic life at Greta Hall, the style of the house and its inmates could have differed very little from Brathay Hall. These two sketches by John Harden may legitimately be used, therefore, as illustrative of interior scenes at the Southey-Coleridge residence during the Laureate's heyday.

Cumbrian speech (picked up at school) was a family joke, was known as "Braet'it" (Braithwaite), while Hartley was always "Job".

The Greta Hall children were lucky in being surrounded by adults who were capable of running an excellent "home grown" schoolroom. Mrs Lovell taught English and Latin; Mrs Coleridge French, Italian, writing, arithmetic and needlework; Southey Spanish and Greek; and Miss Barker, a neighbour, gave instruction in drawing and music. "We keep regular School from ½ past nine until 4 with the exception of an hour for walking and an half hour for dressing," Mrs Coleridge reported to Thomas Poole. "Should we not all be very learned!"

However in the summer, when all the Lakers arrived and life was a non-stop whirl of boating, picnics, parties, excursions, amateur dramatics and musical evenings, Southey was almost "too lenient" in letting the children off school and their studies so that they might enjoy some of the fun. The endless flow of visitors to Greta Hall increased with the years. Poets, painters, prelates, and politicians; lady novelists, academicians, and the aristocracy; old friends, and total strangers, all came to Greta Hall. One day the children would be frisking with the archbishop of London, the next they would be listening to Lord Wilberforce telling them funny stories, and the next they would be watching wide eyed, while George Dawe, the celebrated R.A., set up a vast canvas, nine feet by eight-and-a-half, in Coleridge's old study and set about painting "A woman on the point of a high Rock, taking her infant from an Eagle's Nest; the Eagle flying over her head."

But for much of the time the Greta Hall children forgot all about the grown-ups and amused themselves in their own way. These happy days were recaptured by Sara Coleridge *fille* in verses which, twenty five years later, and with a reputation of her own as scholar and writer, she composed for her little son, Herbert Coleridge.

LODORE

(Southey wrote this poem to answer a nursery query,
"How does the water come down at Lodore?")

. . . Showering and springing,
   Flying and flinging,
   Writhing and ringing,
   Eddying and whisking,
   Spouting and frisking,
   Turning and twisting,
   Around and around
   With endless rebound! . . .
Dizzying and deafening the ear with its sound . . .
   Collecting, projecting,
   Receding and speeding,
   And whizzing and hissing,
   And dripping and skipping,
   And hitting and spitting . . .
And thumping and plumping and bumping and jumping,
And dashing and flashing and splashing and clashing;
And so never ending, but always descending,
Sounds and motions for ever and ever are blending,
All at once and all o'er with a mighty uproar.
And this way the water comes down at Lodore.

Robert Southey
(*"Rhymes for the Nursery", 1820*)

When Herbert's Mama was a slim little Maid,
And liv'd among Waterfalls, Mountains and Lakes,
With Edith her cousin, she rambled and played
And both of them garden'd with spades and with rakes . . .

A wood full of harebells was close to their home,
It led to a River all broken with rocks:
They lov'd o'er the thyme and the heather to roam
'Mid brackens and brambles they ruin'd their frocks;
They tuck'd up their trowsers to paddle and wade,
And washed their Doll's clothes in the water so cold;
They wove pretty garlands within the cool shade –
Their May Pole was beauteous indeed to behold.

In Winter they put on their great wooden Clogs,
And down to the Lake with young Derwent they ran;
The Sun having chased all the vapours and fogs
Their sport on the Ice in high glee they began.
In Summer they gathered the primroses pale
And filled little Baskets with fruits and with flowers;
To make Primrose Wine and their friends to regale
Was one of their pleasures in Summer's gay hours.

And what of Southey as Poet Laureate? Rather than weary ourselves with lengthy excerpts from *The Curse of Kehama*, or *Roderick, Last of the Goths*, or *A Vision of Judgement*, or some such effusion, we may well prefer to divert ourselves with Southey in less ambitious, and therefore far more successful mood. For his and Coleridge's children he wrote nursery verse, including the celebrated effervescent *Lodore*; for his friends he wrote delightfully about his beloved cats.

The artist, William Westall, a great friend of Southey's, frequently visited Greta Hall; here he has produced a highly romantic view of the house, from the north-east, creating the impression that it stands on a richly wooded cliff overhanging a fine river. In reality, its sits on a rather treeless knoll (Southey himself complained of the lack of timber round the house) with the Greta ("Dear domestic stream" as Coleridge cosily called it) babbling behind it and then swinging round in a bend to the north, past (in Southey's day) small mills, market-gardens and hop-fields. However, poetic license is permissible when depicting the Poet Laureate's Lake Country residence! And a large pencil factory, together with Keswick school and a belt of modern houses make it difficult for us nowadays to visualize the landscape immediately surrounding Greta Hall as it was. At least the mountains have not changed!

ROBERT SOUTHEY'S MEMOIR OF THE CATS OF GRETA HALL

In the autumn of the year 1803, when I entered upon this place of abode, I found the hearth in possession of two cats, whom my nephew Hartley Coleridge, (then in the 7th year of his age), had named Lord Nelson and Bona Marietta. The former was an ugly specimen of the streaked-carrotty, but in spite of his complexion, he was altogether a good Cat, affectionate, vigilant, and brave; and for services performed against the Rats was deservedly raised in succession to the rank of Baron, Viscount, and Earl.

Bona Marietta was the mother of Bona Fidelia, so named by my nephew aforesaid. Bona Fidelia left a daughter and a grand-daughter; the former I called Madame Bianchi – the latter Pulcheria. Their fate was extraordinary as well as mournful. When good old Mrs Wilson died, who used to feed and indulge them, they immediately forsook the house, nor could they be allured to enter it again, though they continued to wander and moan around it, and came for food. After some weeks Madame Bianchi disappeared, and Pulcheria soon afterwards died of a disease endemic at that time among cats.

For a considerable time afterwards, an evil fortune attended all our attempts at re-establishing a Cattery. For some time I feared we were at the end of our Cata-a-logue: but at last Fortune, as if to make amends for her late severity, sent us two at once, – the never-to-be-enough-praised Rumpelstilzchen, and the equally-to-be-admired Hurlyburlybuss.

First for the first of these . . . When the Midgeleys went away from the next house, they left this creature to our hospitality, cats being the least moveable of all animals because of their strong local predilections. The change was gradually and therefore easily brought about, for he was already acquainted with the children and with me; and having the same precincts to prowl in was hardly sensible of any other difference in his condition than that of obtaining a name; for when he was consigned to us he was an anonymous cat.

Whence Hurlyburlybuss came was a mystery, and a mystery it long remained. He appeared here, as Mango Capac did in Peru, no one knew from whence. He never attempted to enter the house, frequently disappeared for days, and once, since my return, for so long a time that he was actually believed to be dead and veritably lamented as such. The wonder was whither did he retire at such times – and to whom did he belong; for neither I in my daily walks, nor the children, nor any of the servants, ever by chance saw him anywhere except in our own domain. There was something so mysterious in this, that in old times it might have excited strong suspicion, and he would have been in danger of passing for a Witch in disguise, or a familiar. To this day we are ignorant who has the honour to be his owner in the eye of the law; and the owner is equally ignorant of the high favour in which Hurlyburlybuss is held, of the heroic name which he has obtained, and that his fame has extended far and wide; that with Rumpelstilzchen he has been celebrated in song, by some hitherto undiscovered poet, and that his glory will go down to future generations.

Strong enmity unhappily subsists between these otherwise gentle and most amiable cats . . .

Two stars keep not their motion in one
                                                sphere,
Nor can one purlieu brook a double reign
Of Hurlyburlybuss and Rumpelstilzchen.

The result of many a fierce conflict was, that Hurly remained master of the green and garden, and the whole of the out door premises; Rumpel always upon the appearance of his victorious enemy retiring into the house as a citadel or sanctuary. The conqueror was, perhaps, in part indebted for this superiority to his hardier habits of life, living always in the open air, and providing for himself; while Rumpel, who was kittened with a silver spoon in his mouth, passed his hours in luxurious repose beside the fire, and looked for his meals as punctually as any two-legged member of the family.

Some weeks ago Hurlyburlybuss was manifestly emaciated and enfeebled by ill health, and Rumpelstilzchen with great magnanimity made overtures of peace. The whole progress of the treaty was seen from the parlour window. The caution with which Rumpel made his advances, the sullen dignity with which they were received, their mutual uneasiness when Rumpel, after a slow and wary approach, seated himself whisker-to-whisker with his rival, the mutual agitation of their tails which, though they did not expand with anger, could not be kept still for suspense, and lastly the manner in which Hurly retreated, like Ajax still keeping his face toward his old antagonist, were worthy to have been represented

by that painter who was called the Rafaelle of Cats.

The overture I fear was not accepted as generously as it was made; for no sooner had Hurlyburlybuss recovered strength than hostilities were recommenced with greater violence than ever. Dreadful were the combats which ensued, as their ears, faces and legs bore witness. Oh it is awful to hear the "dreadful note of preparation" with which they prelude their encounters! – the long low growl slowly rises and swells till it becomes a sharp yowl, – and then it is snapped short by a sound which seems as if they were spitting fire and venom at each other. All means of reconciling them and making them understand how goodly a thing it is for cats to dwell together in peace, and what fools they are to quarrel and tear each other, are in vain.

POETIC STANZAS TO THE LAUREATE
BY HIS CATS

Keswick, January 9th.

DEAR MASTER,
    Let our boldness not offend,
If a few lines of duteous love we send;
Nor wonder that we deal in rhyme, for long
We've been familiar with the founts of song . . .
This by the way – we now proceed to tell,
That all within the bounds of home are well;
All but your faithful cats, who inly pine;
The cause your Conscience may too well divine.
Ah! little do you know how swiftly fly
The venomed darts of feline jealousy;
How delicate a task to deal it is
With a Grimalkin's sensibilities,
When Titten's tortoise fur you smoothed with bland
And coaxing courtesies of lip and hand,
We felt as if, (poor Puss's constant dread,)
Some school-boy stroked us both from tail to head;
Nor less we suffer'd while with sportive touch
And purring voice, you played with grey-backed Gutch;
And when with eager step, you left your seat,
To get a peep at Richard's snow-white feet,
Himself all black; we long'd to stop his breath
With something like his royal namesake's death;
If more such scenes our frenzied fancies see,
Resolved we hang from yonder apple tree –
And were not that a sad catastrophe!
O! then return to your deserted lake,
Dry eyes that weep, and comfort hearts that ache;
Our mutual jealousies we both disown,
Content to share, rather than lose a throne.
The Parlour, Rumple's undisputed reign,
Hurley's the rest of all your wide domain,
Return, return, dear Bard, κατ' ἐξοχήν,
Restore the happy days that once have been,
Resign yourself to Home, the Muse and us.
  (*Scratch'd*) Rumpelstilzchen
        Hurlyburlybuss.

Robert Southey

WORDSWORTH'S STRUGGLE AND REWARD

As the years passed, everyone who knew Wordsworth, or anything of him, anticipated hearing that he had started work in earnest on producing *The Recluse* – the great philosophical poem foisted upon him by Coleridge. By 1804 Wordsworth had written a great deal of magnificent poetry designed to slot into *The Recluse*, but it was becoming painfully clear that he was incapable of synthesizing *The Ruined Cottage, Michael, Home At Grasmere* and the rest into one great philosophical work: in other words, incapable of synthesizing his views on Nature, Man and Society. He looked to Coleridge for help, but it was not forthcoming. *The Recluse*, instead of being a great and exciting goal, Wordsworth's *raison d'etre* as a poet, became an exhausting burden, a wearisome task that everyone looked to him to complete, and

which he himself knew could never be completed. In 1814, he published nine books of *The Excursion*, which he subsequently described as a "Portion of the Recluse", but he could do no more.

The sense of frustration, of exhaustion almost, that lurks in so much of Wordsworth's later work is attributable to this tragic knowledge that he had not been able to fulfill the immense demand which Coleridge had made of his genius.

". . . The primal truth
Glimmers through many a superstitious form."

William Wordsworth: "Ecclesiastical Sonnet", IV

In Wordsworth's day the Bronze Age stone circles, monoliths and henge sites, were firmly held to be of druid origin. Wordsworth was fascinated by the druids and even more so by the stones themselves, sensing in them meanings immeasurably profound.

Rydal Mount

reputation) increasingly assumed a weighty dignity of manner. There is a tale told of one Grasmere lady who, invited to dine with the Bard at the home of a mutual friend, exclaimed, "What, dine with Wordsworth! I should as soon think of dining in York Minster!"

In 1812 The Wordsworths had gone from Allan Bank to the old rectory in Grasmere village. Here two of the younger children, Catherine and Thomas, died. The proximity of their graves to the house made the Wordsworths determine on a move and in 1814 they went to Rydal Mount. Here the poet lived for the rest of his life, a span of thirty six years. He continued to write a great deal of poetry, including the *Ecclesiastical Sonnets* and the *Duddon Sonnets*. Although, in actual reality, his poetic powers were fading, it was now that he won greatest acclaim. To quote De Quincey, "Up to 1820 the name of Wordsworth was trampled underfoot; from 1820 to 1830 it was militant; from 1830 to 1835 it has been triumphant." However Keats, who at first idolized Wordsworth, became sadly disillusioned when he called at Rydal Mount. The size, style and prominence of the house shook the young poet, who had supposed Wordsworth to be living in the "rustic simplicity and seclusion" of a small cottage. Even more shattering was the discovery that Wordsworth, absent from home, had gone to Appleby to support Lord Lonsdale, the Tory candidate in a forthcoming General Election!

Indeed, at Rydal Mount Wordsworth gradually became transmuted into the revered Bard who, for Victorian England, represented the virtues that the epoch most valued: a regular church goer; a denunciator of all things *lax*, whose poetry was redolent with high moral tone. He himself (at least by

A PARTY OF LADIES AND GENTLEMEN, seated overlooking Grasmere lake, are being read to by a personage in a frock-coat and top hat; a picture which should be subtitled "Homage to the Bard", for under the circumstances one cannot imagine that they are being regaled with anything other than excerpts from Wordsworth's "Excursion". Note Grasmere church, painted white, as it still was at that time; Allan Bank stands in an elevated position just outside the village. When Allom drew this picture, the Wordsworths were living at Rydal Mount and the Bard had entered upon that period when the name of Wordsworth was triumphant.

Recollection of Jessie & my visit Rd Mt & interview with poor Miss W

JOHN HARDEN inscribed this tragic little sketch, dated 25th August 1842, "Recollection of Jessie and my visit Rd Mt & interview with poor Miss Wordsworth". It shows John and Jessie Harden solicitously tending a devastatingly disordered Dorothy, who is being taken out for a breath of fresh air in her little merlin-carriage through the gardens of Rydal Mount.

Each summer saw more and more visitors flocking to Rydal Mount, some of whom were personal friends, or at least known acquaintances of the Wordsworths, but many (as with the visitors at Greta Hall) came with letters of introduction, or introduced themselves on the strength of mutual acquaintance. Others were simply inquisitive strangers, drawn to the gates of Rydal Mount in the hope of catching a glimpse of the poet and his family. One diversion for these onlookers, we are told, was the appearance of Dorothy Wordsworth being given an airing in her wheeled chair, or little merlin carriage. For, tragically, in the early 1830s Dorothy had succumbed to premature senile dementia, or, as the locals called it, had become "faculty crazed." The interminable loving patience shown by Mary and William in the face of her demented demands and incapacities, and her unsettling disturbances and tantrums, was nothing short of saintly.

THE END OF AN ERA

For the final decades of his life Wordsworth's closest friend was probably Thomas Arnold, famous headmaster of Rugby School and protagonist of Muscular Christianity. In 1832 he had purchased Fox How, under Loughrigg and Wordsworth had superintended the building of the House and laying out of the grounds.

In 1834 Coleridge died in Highgate; having fought and subdued his opium addiction, effected reconciliation with his family, and won international acclaim as writer, poet and philosopher. Wordsworth was moved to an elegiac outburst in his finest vein.

Nor has the rolling year twice measured,
From sign to sign, its steadfast course,
Since every mortal power of Coleridge
Was frozen at its marvellous source;

The rapt One, of the godlike forehead,
The heaven-eyed creature sleeps in earth . . .
"Extemporary Effusion upon the death of James Hogg"

Following Robert Southey's death in 1843 it was inevitable that Wordsworth should become Laureate.

THE RYDAL FALLS ranked amongst the foremost Picturesque attractions of the region, the upper force being viewed from a specially constructed bridge, while the lower force (which was considered the superior in Sublimity) was viewed from a small building with a large, unglazed window which framed the tumbling waterfall.

'LONG TIME A CHILD'

Long time a child, and still a child, when years
Had painted manhood on my cheek, was I—
For yet I lived like one not born to die;
A thriftless prodigal of smiles and tears,
No hope I needed, and I knew no fears.
But sleep, though sweet, is only sleep, and waking,
I waked to sleep no more, at once o'ertaking
The vanguard of my age, with all arrears
Of duty on my back. Nor child, nor man,
Nor youth, nor sage, I find my head is grey,
For I have lost the race I never ran:
A rathe December blights my lagging May;
And still I am a child, tho' I be old,
Time is my debtor for my years untold.

Hartley Coleridge

NOVEMBER

The mellow year is hasting to its close;
The little birds have almost sung their last,
Their small notes twitter in the dreary blast—
That shrill-piped harbinger of early snows;
The patient beauty of the scentless rose,
Oft with the Morn's hoar crystal quaintly glass'd,
Hangs, a pale mourner for the summer past,
And makes a little summer where it grows:
In the chill sunbeam of the faint brief day
The dusky waters shudder as they shine,
The russet leaves obstruct the straggling way
Of oozy brooks, which no deep banks define,
And the gaunt woods, in ragged, scant array,
Wrap their old limbs with sombre ivy twine.

Hartley Coleridge

He now moved into a period of composing *Lines Inscribed in a copy of his Poems sent to the Queen for the Royal Library at Windsor* and *Ode on the Installation of His Royal Highness Prince Albert as Chancellor of The University of Cambridge*. He was going down in a sunset glow of Establishment approbation; but the true poetic star now shining in the Lakes firmament was Hartley Coleridge.

THE INHERITANCE

His life had been a strange and tragic one. Following a brilliant career as undergraduate at Merton College, Oxford, he had been awarded a probationary Fellowship at Oriel College. But drink was his undoing and the Fellowship had been withdrawn from him. Thereafter he had lived a shiftless existence; first in London, then in the Lakes. He received a small allowance from his family, eked out with a little unsuccessful school-mastering and some much admired, but financially unrewarding, authorship. His chief reputation was as a poet and from his pen sprang, expecially, some wonderful sonnets – the best of which have quietly taken their place in the annals of English poetry. That he did not become as widely recognized as he should have been is possibly

because, as a character, he represented everything that the Victorian era shuddered from, and furthermore his family and friends made sure that he remained buried deep in the Lake Country, "Out of sight, out of mind."

Not that he wasn't accepted socially; on the contrary, he was a great favourite with many of the most respectable hostesses in the Lakes, but this was because they were careful not to learn where and how he spent much of his time. For he was as at home with the native population as with elegant offcomes.

His odd little figure, stunted and waif-like; his childlike simplicity of manner and irresistible sense

THE NAB, a cottage standing beside Rydal Water, below Nab Scar, was the place where Hartley Coleridge lodged in the final years of his life and where he died. For a while, De Quincey owned the Nab, it having come to his wife, Peggy Simpson, through her mother, but he also inherited enormous debts with the house and was forced to sell it to William Richardson and his wife, who moved in with their lodger, Hartley. Here he wrote some of his finest sonnets, and here Branwell Brontë came to visit him in 1840, for an afternoon of talk. He wrote to Hartley afterwards: "You will, perhaps, have forgotten me, but it will be long before I forget my first conversation with a man of real intellect, in my first visit to the classic lakes of Westmorland."

THE DESERTED CHURCH

A prophecy, the fulfilment of which the writer
never wishes to see.

———————

After long travail on my pilgrimage,
I sat me down beside an aged heap,
For so it seem'd, with one square shatter'd keep,
Pensively frowning on the wrecks of age.
The river there, as at its latest stage,
Sinks in the verdure of its Sunday sleep,
And sings an under-song for them that weep
O'er the sad blots in life's too open page.
I look'd within, but all within was cold!
The walls were mapp'd with isles of dusky damp,
The long stalls look'd irreverently old,
The rush-strewn aisle was like a wither'd swamp,
And mark'd with loitering foot's unholy tramp;
The chancel floor lay thick with sluggish mould.

Hark! do you hear the dull unfrequent knell,
Survivor sad of many a merry peal,
Whose Sabbath music wont to make us feel
Our spirits mounting with its joyous swell,
That scaled the height, that sunk into the dell?
Now lonely, lowly swinging to and fro,
It warns a scatter'd flock e'en yet to go,
And take a sip of the deserted well.
And, dost thou hear?—then, hearing, long endure.
The Gospel sounds not now so loud and bold
As once it did. Some lie in sleep secure,
And many faint because their love is cold;
But never doubt that God may still be found,
Long as one bell sends forth a Gospel sound!

Hartley Coleridge

SONG

———————

She not fair to outward view
    As many maidens be,
Her loveliness I never knew
    Until she smil'd on me;
Oh! then I saw her eye was bright,
A well of love, a spring of light.

But now her looks are coy and cold,
    To mine they ne'er reply,
And yet I cease not to behold
    The love-light in her eye:
Her very frowns are fairer far,
Than smiles of other maidens are.

Hartley Coleridge

REASONS FOR NOT WRITING IN DECEMBER 1842

———————

The sadden'd year has but few days to live
And now seems mourning for its own decay,
What merry rhyme should a poor Poet give
Fit for a maid so innocent and gay.

When winter glitters all with sunny frost
And chrystal gems are hung on every branch
And morning blades with powdery rime embost
Crisply beneath light footsteps crackling cranch;

When streets and roads ring sharp below the wheel
And the flat lake appears a marble floor
And shooting—arrow swift on shoes of steel
The skaters wake blithe echo from the shore;

Then may a bard, though haply stiff and old,
Earn with a jocund verse a lassy's kiss—
But what can I do that have got a cold
On such a muggy, mizzling morn as this?

Hartley Coleridge

TO A CAT

———————

Nelly, methinks, 'twixt thee and me
There is a kind of sympathy;
And could we interchange our nature,—
If I were cat, thou human creature,—
I should, like thee, be no great mouser,
And thou, like me, no great composer;
For, like thy plaintive mews, my muse
With villainous whine doth fate abuse,
Because it hath not made me sleek
As golden down on Cupid's cheek;
And yet thou canst upon the rug lie,
Stretch'd out like snail, or curl'd up snugly,
As if thou wert not lean or ugly;
And I, who in poetic flights
Sometimes complain of sleepless nights,
Regardless of the sun in heaven,
Am apt to dose till past eleven,—
The world would just the same go round
If I were hang'd and thou wert drown'd;
There is one difference, 'tis true,—
Thou does not know it, and I do.

Hartley Coleridge

WORDSWORTH with Hartley Coleridge at Rydal; after a sketch from the life made in 1844, by Mulcaster. Hartley's mother, now living with her daughter in Regent's Park, London, devoted herself to keeping Hartley equipped with a decent wardrobe, but as this sketch shows, he preferred to look derelict. A contemporary recalled "L'al Hartley" exactly as drawn here: "His trousers . . . generally too long, doubled half-way up his leg . . . His hat brushed the wrong way . . . and his look wild, unshaven, weather-beaten."

THE SMALL CELANDINE

There is a Flower, the lesser Celandine,
That shrinks, like many more, from cold and rain;
And, the first moment that the sun may shine,
Bright as the sun himself, 'tis out again!

When hailstones have been falling, swarm on swarm,
Or blasts the green field and the trees distrest,
Oft have I seen it muffled up from harm,
In close self-shelter, like a Thing at rest.

But lately, one rough day, this Flower I passed
And recognised it, though an altered form,
Now standing forth an offering to the blast,
And buffeted at will by rain and storm.

I stopped, and said with inly-muttered voice,
'It doth not love the shower, nor seek the cold:
This neither is its courage nor its choice,
But its necessity in being old.

'The sunshine may not cheer it, nor the dew;
It cannot help itself in its decay;
Stiff in its members, withered, changed of hue.'
And, in my spleen, I smiled that it was grey.

To be a Prodigal's Favourite—then, worse truth,
A Miser's Pensioner—behold our lot!
O Man, that from thy fair and shining youth
Age might but take the things Youth needed not!

William Wordsworth

PERSUASION

'Man's life is like a Sparrow, mighty King!
That—while at banquet with your Chiefs you sit
Housed near a blazing fire — is seen to flit
Safe from the wintry tempest. Fluttering,
Here did it enter; there, on hasty wing,
Flies out, and passes on from cold to cold;
But whence it came we know not, nor behold
Whither it goes. Even such, that transient Thing,
The human Soul; not utterly unknown
While in the Body lodged, her warm abode;
But from what world She came, what woe or weal
On her departure waits, no tongue hath shown;
This mystery if the Stranger can reveal,
His be a welcome cordially bestowed!'

William Wordsworth

TO A CHILD

Small service is true service while it lasts:
Of humblest Friends, bright Creature! scorn not one:
The Daisy, by the shadow that it casts,
Protects the lingering dew-drop from the Sun.

William Wordsworth

of fun made "l'aal Hartley", as they called him, a prime favourite with all the cottagers, the farmers and shepherds, the hunting folk; nor did they fail to appreciate his spellbinding conversation powers: "Aye, l'aal Hartley; he was a phee-losopher!" Every now and again he vanished into the hills on drinking

THE WORDSWORTH GRAVES, Grasmere churchyard. In the front row, from left to right: William Wordsworth ("Willy"), the poet's youngest child, and his wife Fanny (née Graham); Dorothy Wordsworth; a memorial stone to sailor John Wordsworth; William and Mary Wordsworth; their daughter Dora, and Edward Quillianan, whose second wife she became in 1841. On the left of the second row are the headstones of the children, Catherine and Thomas Wordsworth; while behind the central memorial stone is the celtic cross marking Hartley Coleridge's grave.

sprees and was a favourite and renowned "regular" at shepherds' meets and "murry neets" when, his tiny figure perched on some high stool, he would tell marvellously comic tales, recite long scurrilous ballads of his own composition (bringing in local characters and gossip in a salty, witty fashion that brought the house down) and singing songs, also of his own composition. He would carry on all night, until at last, too drunk to remain upright any longer, he would fall off his stool and be deposited in some quiet, warm corner, by those of his friends still able to pick him up and carry him. A fortnight or so later he would turn up at some eminently respectable evening party in Ambleside or Clappersgate; he appeared immaculately, almost elegantly groomed; his manners "old fashioned but perfect, his personality eccentric, but delightful," as one hostess nostalgically recalled, following his death in 1849, the victim of pneumonia resulting from having spent the night dead drunk in a ditch in bitter January.

White-headed almost before he was middle-aged, he was once described as a being "whose head was midwinter, while his heart was green as May." His charm, his wit, his touching sense of personal tragedy, show clearly in his poems.

The Wordsworths had known and loved Hartley since his infancy, and had continued to love him, and stand by him, in his tragic later years. His death occurred a mere eighteen months after that of Wordsworth's beloved daughter Dora. She had been buried in Grasmere churchyard in a plot on the bank of the Rothay; a plot in which it was intended that the Wordsworths, in due course, should all lie together as a family. After Hartley's death Wordsworth gave instructions, "Let him lie as near us as possible . . . It would have been his wish."

A year later Wordsworth himself died, and was buried near Dora. Dorothy followed him to the grave five years later; Mary died in 1859 and joined the family group. These graves today are visited yearly by tens of thousands of people; some merely curious, but others in sincerest homage.

CHAPTER THREE

THE LIVING TRADITION

The Victorians preserved Wordsworth's memory surrounded by the proverbial odour of sanctity. Much of his earlier poetry lay unread and sedulously neglected. A firm decision had been taken by everyone, it seemed, to maintain the legend that Wordsworth had been born a middle-aged man, who had bypassed youth and its indiscretions and wild oats – had never been anything but an exemplary husband and father, and a Tory pillar of Church and State.

By far and away his most successful work, in terms of readership, was his *Guide to the Lakes*, first published in 1810 and chief rival to West's hoary, but still highly esteemed, *Guide* of 1778. Matthew Arnold (son of Dr Thomas Arnold) was fond of telling the story of a clergyman who, having enthused over Wordsworth's *Guide*, went on to ask if the author had written anything else?

Wordsworth's *Guide* took it for granted that tourists would travel in their own carriages; every now and again the author briskly advised a short walk if some view or other were to be properly seen and appreciated. It was not enough for visitors to be "contented with what they can collect with their eyes from the barouch box or from the seat of the open

Landau". They must make an effort, "aspire at something beyond a superficial entertainment . . . The Soul of objects must be communicated with."

This was the kind of elevated sermonizing that Victorians enjoyed. But in the end it might be said that Wordsworth defeated himself, with his constant admonitions to walk. In the latter part of the nineteenth century more and more people took to walking and the favourite guidebook now was M.J.B. Baddeley's *The Lake District*, described by the great H.H. Symonds as "the best workaday guide for the

walker which has ever been written." Mountford John Baddeley, B.A., lived at Windermere and was himself an indefatigable walker. He surpassed himself at the time of Queen Victoria's Diamond Jubilee when, in charge of the organization of the District's celebrative beacon fires, he climbed Scafell Pike four times in the course of the great day. Although a workaday guide Baddeley, like a good Victorian, kept a respectful eye on the Bard and did not hesitate to tell readers firmly, that, "The first thing one does in Grasmere is to visit Wordsworth's grave."

KESWICK BOAT-LANDINGS: ". . . something beyond a superficial entertainment", (Wordsworth's "Guide to the Lakes"). Over the past two centuries, thousands of holiday makers have hired boats from this little bay, set between Cockshot Wood and Crow Park, and have rowed out to savour the Romantic delights of Derwent Water under a sunset sky.

Grasmere from Helm Crag by W. Heaton Cooper. A keen mountaineer, Heaton Cooper has illustrated all the Lake District rock climbing guides and was one of the first artists to paint his native mountains from the higher levels. He is a member of the Royal Institute of Painters in Watercolours and for eleven years was president of the Lake Artist's Society. His home, studio and gallery are in Grasmere.

The close of the Victorian era saw the end of veneration for the Bard of Rydal Mount. Over the ensuing decades Wordsworth's admirers dwindled to a small, select group of persons associated in the popular mind with beards, sandals, vegetarianism and teetotalism: the Bardic tradition of plain living and high thinking. The Wordsworth "backlash" was succinctly encapsulated by Max Beerbohm's famous

cartoon of Wordsworth and the little maid of *We are Seven*. Picturesque Tourists no longer came to the Lakes, which increasingly became the playground of the English professional classes who went there to walk and rock-climb. The more scholarly of these would sometimes carry a copy of *The Prelude* in their capacious pockets.

WORDSWORTH'S INFLUENCE PERSISTS

In 1933 H.H. Symonds, champion of the then infant Youth Hostels Association, the Friends of the Lake District, and an early campaigner for a National Park, published his classic work, *Walking in the Lake District*, still esteemed by the *cognoscente* as the leading guide for serious Lake District walkers: an unparalleled combination of practical guide and penetrative erudition. Symonds himself was profoundly influenced by Wordsworth's *Guide to the Lakes*, and *The Prelude*. He took it for granted that his readers were not only capable of walking a good twenty-five to thirty miles a day when "walked in", but would be also Wordsworthians, and that their Wordsworth would be the poet and man of pre-1814 vintage. Dove Cottage, said Symonds, should be visited because it was there that "in 1804—5 Wordsworth wrote most of his greatest poetry in the Prelude ... where he flings the gates of his heart wide open, and reaches to the every depth and height of speech and understanding."

When it came to discussion of local architecture, or sheep and shepherding, or formation of the mountains, or problems of afforestation, or protecting the landscape, Symonds turned unhestitatingly to Wordsworth. It would be no exaggeration to say that Symonds, guided extensively by Wordsworth, may correctly be seen as a salient shaping influence upon the Lake District of today.

A foremost work on the Lakes since Symonds is *The Lake District: A Landscape History*, by W.H. Pearsall and Winifred Pennington, published in 1973. The authors make no secret of their extensive debt to Wordsworth's *Guide* (and quote Professor W.G. Hoskins' opinion that it is "one of the best guide books ever written"). The overall conclusion of the Pearsall–Pennington study is that Wordsworth has been, and remains, the greatest, most reliable and enlightened of conservationists, whose wisdom, if consulted, must help preserve the "fells and dales in their present beauty."

Today's Dove Cottage Museum assists in presenting Wordsworth, at least partly, in this role: thereby effectively preventing him from popularly being seen merely as a tourist attraction, or obsolete relic.

Dove Cottage was originally purchased by a private philanthropist in the 1860s, with a view to its becoming a species of Wordsworth Museum-cum-shrine in the not too distant future. However it was not until 1890 that a Dove Cottage Trust was founded,

DOVE COTTAGE as it appears today. The cottage is open to visitors all the year round and is maintained in almost its original condition by the Wordsworth Trust.

by the Reverend Stopford Brooke, chaplain to Queen Victoria. The cottage was opened to the public the following year. From the first it was intended that, in addition to public viewing of the cottage, an important collection of MSS material would be assembled and housed in a library where serious scholars would be able to work. These aims have been achieved. Some 60,000 people visit the cottage and museum each year; meanwhile, in the privacy of the library, distinguished scholars from many parts of the world work on the ever growing collection of manuscripts,

particularly the early versions of the poems, which have come more and more to be acclaimed as some of Wordsworth's finest work.

REACHING BEYOND POETRY

Coleridge's influence upon posterity has been considerably more extensive than that of Wordsworth; chiefly because his mind was immeasurably more far-reaching, but partly because his life and interests were not confined to the Lakes. His influence has been strongly felt upon literary and art criticism; aesthetics; dialectics; philosophy; theology; psychology; education; scientific hypotheses; political theory, and, of course, developments in prose writing and poetry.

Our chief interest here and now must be in how the pervasive influence of that full flowering of English Romanticism, when Coleridge and Wordsworth were working together on poetry and prose that saw "into the heart of things", changed the way in which modern man looks at, and feels about the natural world, and man in relation to that world, and how this is reflected in the work of succeeding poets and painters.

INSPIRATION FROM THE LAKES

The Lake District continued, and continues, to play an important role in stimulating poets and painters to look, and see, and by pursuing to their logical conclusion the principles of realism in the depiction of nature in writing and painting thereby to open up the imagination to deeper insights into the real world – to paraphrase John Ruskin, artist, critic, poet, author, and social reformer, upon whose shoulders the mantle of the Lake Poets fell. Ruskin carried on the tradition of extending insight into the synthesis of Nature, Man and Society. This was something that Tennyson, who succeeded Wordsworth as Laureate, had never aspired to do, despite the fact that he knew and loved the Lakes, having first come there in the 1830s as a Cambridge undergraduate, to stay as guest of his friend James Spedding, the Francis Bacon scholar, at Mirehouse, Bassenthwaite.

DUDDON VALLEY by Eric Gilboy. Gilboy began work under the tutelage of Ivan Sanderson and Barton Thomas in decorative fabric design; he ultimately became director of the design teams of Courtauld's, Edinburgh Weavers and Morton Sundour, before retiring early to concentrate on his first love, painting. For the past twenty five years he has lived in the Lake District, with his studio in Thornthwaite, near Keswick; his great admiration is for Turner and like Turner, Gilboy paints in mixed media, but with his own eye for what he sees in the Lakes landscape.

"There is a hurry in his sketch. The cloud
will only stay a while like that
before a serious change obliterates.
A cloud will not stay quiet: it burns
and draws in all that is around,
cusping and reeling across Old Man of Coniston."

David Scott: "Ruskin's 'Sketches from Nature' "

Spedding, together with Tennyson and Tennyson's friend Arthur Hallam, were all Trinity College men and members of the famous group known as the Cambridge Apostles. The visit to Mirehouse was organized as a reading and literary discussion party, pursuits which chiefly took place in the Mirehouse smoking-room, well away from the ladies. The Mirehouse circle (which attracted men as important, and as diverse, as Robert Southey and Thomas Carlyle), was a notable feature of literary life during the 1830s and '40s. There was never, of course, a smoking-room at Rydal Mount (though, as we know, during Coleridge's day at Greta Hall there had been poetic pipe smoking in his study). When Tennyson appeared in Keswick in late 1850 on his honeymoon

en route, with his bride (née Emily Sellwood), for a stay at Mirehouse, respectable Keswickians, accustomed to Southey and Wordsworth (they had long since put Coleridge out of their minds) were deeply shocked by the newly assigned Laureate who trailed not clouds of glory, but tobacco smoke, through which might be glimpsed a swirl of cape, sombrero and flying mane.

When Tennyson died in 1892 the Laureateship would have been offered to Ruskin, but for the fact that he had gone out of his mind. Ruskin (1819–1900) wrote little, if any, noteworthy verse, but his "poetic prose" was enormously widely read and admired, and he certainly saw the role of poet as Wordsworth had seen it. In 1859 Ruskin wrote in conferred as much as ever the loveliest or saddest of Camelot."

In 1843 Ruskin's first volume of *Modern Painters* won him enthusiastic acclaim from many distinguished elders, including Wordsworth, who was deeply impressed by it. He followed this with *The Seven Lamps of Architecture, The Stones of Venice, The Elements of Drawing*, and the autobiographical *Praeterita, Unto This Last* (a study in political economy which revealed him as the prophet of a new social consciousness) and *The Bible of Amiens* (a marvellous study of Amiens cathedral which Proust so admired that he translated it into French), to single out but the better known of his writings. His own sketches and paintings were highly esteemed in his day and become increasingly admired with the passage of time.

His passion for beauty, and what he called "detailed truth to nature", coupled with an exceptional power of analysis, at times approaching that of Coleridge himself, had a profound effect not only upon art, which he saw as engaging the whole of human personality, but upon the concept of society itself. In pursuing his chosen career of dedication to looking, seeing, and analysis of what he saw, and resultantly felt, Ruskin brought Wordsworth and Coleridge's "seeing into the life of things" into full prominence as a viable intellectual, cultural and social concept.

THESE INFORMAL SKETCHES by James Spedding of Tennyson (above) and Hallam (right), show them in a relaxed mood in the Mirehouse smoking-room. The two were inseparable friends. Hallam became engaged to Tennyson's sister Emily and stayed frequently with the family at their rectory home, Somersby; a happy period in the lives of both young men, during which Tennyson made remarkable strides as a poet, producing, in 1832 at the age of twenty three, the volume of "Poems" which established his reputation. A year later he was devastated by Hallam's death from tuberculosis. Visitors to Mirehouse can see the celebrated smoking-room, and catch whiffs of elusive tobacco and echoes of literary talk and laughter.

critical vein to Tennyson on the subject of the latter's first series in *Idylls of the King* (the Arthurian *opus* upon which Tennyson worked for over thirty years), saying that a poet's true task was "the unerring transcript of . . . actuality . . . the relation of a story of any real human life . . . I have seen faces, and heard voices, by road and street-side, which claimed or

A LITERARY INHERITANCE

In 1867 Ruskin purchased Brantwood on the eastern shore of Coniston Water, originally an old farmhouse and for a while the home of William James Linton, a distinguished artist and wood-engraver who was also a dedicated republican and fiery political writer; a zealous Chartist and friend and follower of Mazzini.

After several adventures in radical journalism Linton set up his own printing press at Brantwood in an outhouse (still to be seen) on the walls of which he painted slogans. "God and the People" proclaim heavy letters still staring across the room which once housed his printing press, from which copies of his monthly paper, *The English Republic*, emerged in rotation, to be parcelled up and carted across the fells to Windermere station. A troop of little Lintons, boys and girls all dressed excactly the same, in long blue flannel blouses and round straw hats, with bloomers under the blouses, played in the garden.

Linton's second wife was Eliza Lynn, pioneer woman journalist and daughter of the rector of Crosthwaite, Keswick. As a girl she had been much admired by Hartley Coleridge. In 1863 she and Linton together produced their beautiful guidebook, *The Lake Country*, wholly Wordsworthian in approach and spirit. Later Linton and his wife parted company; he went to America with his children, Eliza Linton stayed in England and continued her journalism, but they remained good friends and in their frequent correspondence often referred to the happy days they had shared at Brantwood; now the home of Ruskin, seated in his study writing, or at his window jotting analytical studies of the clouds over Coniston Old Man, or sketching them.

THE IDYLLIC LITTLE CHURCH of St. Bega, dating back to the twelfth century, stands in its simple pastoral churchyard on the eastern shore of Bassenthwaite Lake. The church is said to have been in Tennyson's mind when, in his version of the "Morte d'Arthur", he described how Sir Bedivere, the last of Arthur's knights, bore the king's body to "a chapel in the fields" on the verge of "a great water". Certainly, Tennyson must have known the church of St. Bega well, for it stands only a short distance from Mirehouse, where he used to stay when visiting the Lakes.

During his years at Coniston, Ruskin had as his secretary-companion W.G. Collingwood, who had been one of his most brilliant students in the days when Ruskin had been Slade Professor at Oxford, and who himself became author, historian, archaeologist and antiquarian, in all these fields contributing greatly to study and understanding of the Lakes. His book *The Lake Counties*, published in 1932, and described by Hugh Walpole as containing some of the "grandest prose writing about the Lake District in existence" reveals an unmistakable debt to Wordsworthian looking and feeling within the context of the landscape, and was to become an influence upon subsequent conservationist thinking. Collingwood also has another claim to fame, inasmuch as he was the grandfather of Ransome's Swallows in *Swallows and Amazons*. And lastly, but by no means least, he was an exceptionally fine painter; being described by W. Heaton Cooper as, "The first painter in the Lake District who went up into the hills, and painted what he saw up there, and not from below."

THE MODERN PERSPECTIVE

Of the poets whose poems form the conclusion of this book, only one cannot, geographically, be described as connected with the Lakes: Robert Frost, the New England poet. Yet he, of all modern poets, may most truly be described as Wordsworthian. His voice reaches us from the other side of the Atlantic; a long way away from Grasmere, as terrestial distance goes, but in terms of poetry a mere two feet away, or less; noting the texture of leaves; the movement of the wind; watching a mountain,

> I felt it like a wall
> Behind which I was sheltered from a wind.
>
> *"The Mountain"*

JOHN RUSKIN in his study at Brantwood, by W.G. Collingwood. Many of Ruskin's famous cloud studies were painted from this study window overlooking Coniston Lake, with the Old Man of Coniston beyond. Brantwood, today, is open to the public, with much of Ruskin's own furniture in place as it was in his lifetime; a fine collection of his paintings are on display throughout the house.

THE TUFT OF FLOWERS

I went to turn the grass once after one
Who mowed it in the dew before the sun.

The dew was gone that made his blade so keen
Before I came to view the leveled scene.

I looked for him behind an isle of trees;
I listened for his whetstone on the breeze.

But he had gone his way, the grass all mown,
And I must be, as he had been,—alone,

'As all must be,' I said within my heart,
'Whether they work together or apart.'

But as I said it, swift there passed me by
On noiseless wing a bewildered butterfly,

Seeking with memories grown dim o'er night
Some resting flower of yesterday's delight.

And once I marked his flight go round and round,
As where some flower lay withering on the ground.

And then he flew as far as eye could see,
And then on tremulous wing came back to me.

I thought of questions that have no reply,
And would have turned to toss the grass to dry;

But he turned first, and led my eye to look
At a tall tuft of flowers beside a brook,

A leaping tongue of bloom the scythe had spared
Beside a reedy brook the scythe had bared.

The mower in the dew had loved them thus,
By leaving them to flourish, not for us,

Nor yet to draw one thought of ours to him,
But from sheer morning gladness at the brim.

The butterfly and I had lit upon,
Nevertheless, a message from the dawn,

That made me hear the wakening birds around,
And hear his long scythe whispering to the ground,

And feel a spirit kindred to my own;
So that henceforth I worked no more alone;

But glad with him, I worked as with his aid,
And weary, sought at noon with him the shade;

And dreaming, as it were, held brotherly speech
With one whose thought I had not hoped to reach.

'Men work together,' I told him from the heart,
'Whether they work together or apart.'

Robert Frost

POETS AND PAINTERS TODAY

Robert Frost (1874–1963) spent the three most important formulative years of his development as a poet in England (1912–1915), during which time he came deeply under the influence of Wordsworth. His poems, though almost always about New England, where he lived the greater part of his life, bear a strong understrain of Wordsworthian feeling and response: as in the narrative poems about the basic emotions and relationships of New England country folk, poems in which the presence of countryside itself is always powerful and together with the seasons and elements plays a salient part in the dreams, and shorter, brilliant and beautiful lyrical poems, with their reflective comments upon Man,

"On the mountain's brow the shadow of a hand."

David Wright: "In what we call good weather"

Cooper and Eric Gilboy, he is one of today's artists who has a special gift for "seeing into the life of things" in the Lake Country.

South African born David Wright, a poet and author of great distinction comes from Scots descent, his grandfather having been quarry master at Annan, Dumfrieshire. Deaf since the age of seven, Wright came to England at the age of fourteen to receive deaf schooling, later going to Oxford University. He held the Gregory Fellowship at Leeds, 1965–67. He lives and works in Cumbria, but spends a good deal of his time abroad. A Wordsworth scholar and kken fell-walker, his understanding of Romanticism and of the Lake District gives his poetry a quality that is simultaneously timeless, and intensely contemporary.

Norman Nicholson, born in Millom, Cumbria in 1914, was the region's most celebrated modern poet. He made no attempt to conceal his debt to Wordsworth and many of his most famous poems pursue and extend Wordsworth's principal themes.

David Scott (b. 1947), one of the finest of today's generation of poets, writes about shepherds with clear Wordsworthian insight:

"You can tell that here is neither love nor money" but the old game fathers have taught sons to win."

Echo of Michael and Luke! Scott knows much of flocks; he is vicar of Torpenhow (Trepenna), lying on the rim of the Carlisle plain behind Skidda (in local parlance, "back'arreyatt" – back of the gate); a deeply Cumbrian part of the world.

Geoffrey Holloway – "to practise is to look" – has an eye and a philosophy fundamentally Coleridgean. Born in 1918, he passed his childhood in Shropshire. During the last war, he served with the Sixth Airborne Parachute Regiment, Field Ambulance. After the war, he made his home in Kendal and became a mental welfare officer for Westmorland County Council. His poetry is a significant example of today's extension of the work initially done by William, Dorothy and Coleridge in the business of looking and seeing and the involvement of Imagination.

Sidney Keyes, whose "In Memoriam" is a deeply moving tribute to the poet, died in action in the Second World War.

Nature and Society, as in "The Tuft of Flowers".

John Lacoux, whose painting of Overdale Farm accompanies this poem, was born in 1930 of a French father and an English mother, and is a dedicated Wordsworthian who spends much of his time painting in Cumbria. Many of his strongly Romantic pictures are directly inspired by images from Wordsworth's poems. Together with William Heaton

IN WHAT WE CALL GOOD WEATHER

That afternoon, in what we call good weather,
There was a cloud at anchor in the sky
Above a mountain basking lazily
Like leviathan; both of them together
Obeying probable laws without error
In benign transmutation of energy;
These gentle phenomena announced July,
A stone mountain with a cloud in tether.

By the hazard of their station on that day
While the undarkened valley spread around,
The sun, interpreting water and the land,
Drew from their coincidence an image
When like a negative of the cloud it laid
On the mountain's brow the shadow of a hand.

David Wright

IN MEMORIAM
WILLIAM WORDSWORTH

No room for mourning: he's gone out
Into the noisy glen, or stands between the stones
Of the gaunt ridge, or you'll hear his shout
Rolling among the screes, he being a boy again.
He'll never fail nor die,
And if they laid his bones
In the wet vaults or iron sarcophagi
Of fame, he'd rise at the first summer rain
And stride across the hills to seek
His rest among the broken lands and clouds.
He was a stormy day, a granite peak
Spearing the sky; and look, about its base
Words flower like crocuses in the hanging woods,
Blank though the dalehead and the bony face.

Sidney Keyes

CLOUDED HILLS

Though you can't see them,
You know that they are there.

Beneath the Herdwick fleece of mist,
You can feel the heave of the hill.

You can sense the tremor of old volcanoes,
Tense with damped-down fire.

Under a white meringue of cumulus,
Or behind the grey rain-break of a winter's day.

You are aware of the pikes straining high above you,
Spiking up to an unseen sky.

Norman Nicholson

FLANKING SHEEP IN MOSEDALE

All summer the sheep were strewn like crumbs
across the fell, until the bracken turned brittle
and it was time they were gathered
into the green patchwork of closer fields.
Dogs and men sweep a whole hillside in minutes
save for the stray, scared into a scramble
up a gully. A dog is detached: whistled off
by the shepherd, who in one hand
holds a pup straining at the baling twine
and in the other a crook, light as a baton.
His call cuts the wind across the tarn:
it is the voice of the first man who
booted it across this patch to bring
strays to the place where he would have them.
You can tell that here is neither love nor money
but the old game fathers have taught sons to win.
You can see it is done well, when the dogs
lie panting, and the sheep encircled dare not move.

David Scott

182

THE OPTICS OF HOLISM

To split the eye three ways, see
conclusively the wind turn
a sycamore leaf to a white star,
a silver birch to a corral of manes,
yet in the same flashed breath defer
to the branched indifference of a clock—
this is spontaneously to cry
for single dedication: either
to kneel down before the hope of Light,
ride the wild present like a brave, bareback,
or settle for design in
Roman inches, equably . . .

Yet, to be whole, one is required to conjure
all three, expressly fuse
their grained autonomies . . .

Difficult. Yet, imperative to keep
mid-eye its blazing possibility;
in a star-spurred second
the heart's unearthly centaur
giving immortal presence
to the timed, pragmatic hoop.

And though such triple magic's
the unlikeliest constellation—
to practise is to look.

Geoffrey Holloway

LIST OF ILLUSTRATIONS

INDEX

Figures in **bold type** are poetry
references
Figures in *italic type* are illustration
references

ACKNOWLEDGMENTS

The author and the publishers would like to extend their grateful thanks to the following persons and organizations:

David Lyons and Karen Kirkby, Event Horizons, Ambleside; Mrs. Joan Coleridge; Rosemary Hoggarth and the Wordsworth Trust, Dove Cottage; Mike Francis and the National Library of Wales; Richard Wordsworth; Dr. S.T. Chapman and the Armitt Library; Mrs. Eileen Jay, Chairman of the Armitt Trust; Felicity Owen; the Brantwood Trustees; John Spedding; Cressida Pemberton-Pigott; John Dawson of the Ruskin Museum, Coniston; the Colnterbrook Trus-

tees; John Gerrish; Victoria A.J. Slowe and the Abbot Hall Art Gallery, Kendal; Laura Hamilton of Carlisle Museums and Art Gallery; Judith Collieu of Leicestershire Museums, Art Galleries & Record Service; Judith Prendergast, National Portrait Gallery, London; S.T. Galloway, National Gallery, London; Norman Ackroyd; John Lacoux; Eric Gilboy; John C. Heaton Cooper and the Heaton Cooper Studio, Grasmere; the Mary Evans Picture Library; Mary Moorman; R.E. Alton; George Bott; Warren Elsby; Cumbrian County Library, especially the staff of the Keswick branch; Jonathan Wordsworth; Sheila Watson of Watson & Little Ltd., London.

ACKNOWLEDGMENTS

The author and the publishers would like to extend their grateful thanks to the following persons and organizations:

David Lyons and Karen Kirkby, Event Horizons, Ambleside; Mrs. Joan Coleridge; Rosemary Hoggarth and the Wordsworth Trust, Dove Cottage; Mike Francis and the National Library of Wales; Richard Wordsworth; Dr. S.T. Chapman and the Armitt Library; Mrs. Eileen Jay, Chairman of the Armitt Trust; Felicity Owen; the Brantwood Trustees; John Spedding; Cressida Pemberton-Pigott; John Dawson of the Ruskin Museum, Coniston; the Colnterbrook Trustees; John Gerrish; Victoria A.J. Slowe and the Abbot Hall Art Gallery, Kendal; Laura Hamilton of Carlisle Museums and Art Gallery; Judith Collieu of Leicestershire Museums, Art Galleries & Record Service; Judith Prendergast, National Portrait Gallery, London; S.T. Galloway, National Gallery, London; Norman Ackroyd; John Lacoux; Eric Gilboy; John C. Heaton Cooper and the Heaton Cooper Studio, Grasmere; the Mary Evans Picture Library; Mary Moorman; R.E. Alton; George Bott; Warren Elsby; Cumbrian County Library, especially the staff of the Keswick branch; Jonathan Wordsworth; Sheila Watson of Watson & Little Ltd., London.